20 WAYS TO BE MORE CREATIVE IN YOUR JOB

Bob Weinstein

FIRESIDE

A Fireside Book
Published by Simon & Schuster, Inc.
New York

Also by Bob Weinstein:
Resumes For Hard Times

For Bonnie

Copyright © 1983 by Bob Weinstein
All rights reserved
including the right of reproduction
in whole or in part in any form
A Fireside Book
Published by Simon & Schuster, Inc.
Simon & Schuster Building
Rockefeller Center
1230 Avenue of the Americas
New York, New York 10020

FIRESIDE and colophon are registered trademarks of Simon & Schuster, Inc.

Designed by Stone Associates

Manufactured in the United States of America

Printed and bound by Fairfield Graphics

1 2 3 4 5 6 7 8 9 10

Library of Congress Cataloging in Publication Data

Weinstein, Bob, date.
 20 ways to be more creative in your job.

 "A Fireside book."
 1. Job enrichment. 2. Creative ability in business.
I. Title. II. Title: Twenty ways to be more creative
in your job.
HF5549.5.J616W46   1983   650.1   83-17502
ISBN 0-671-47193-7

CONTENTS

Acknowledgments

Putting this project together was a creative effort in itself. I'd like to thank the following people for providing information and assistance and for keeping my creative wheels humming efficiently throughout the project: Dr. Don Ely, Director of Personnel Services of Nabisco Brands Inc.; Mariana Somer, President of Creative Communication Corporation; Dr. E. P. Torrance, of the University of Georgia, for letting me use his Creative Motivation Scale; my editor, Barbara Gess, for guidance and constructive criticism; Josh Weinstein, for spending countless hours in the library researching the subject; Jenny Weinstein, for tirelessly tieing the information together; Bonnie Weinstein, for inspiration; and, last but not least, my colleague and pal, T. Pete Bonner.

INTRODUCTION

You too can be creative in your work. "Not me!" you say, hesitantly. "I'm not creative. Only painters, poets, writers, and composers are creative." All of the above skills require a creative mind. But so do the skills of technicians, advertising people, public relations workers, computer operators, industrial supervisors, systems analysts, accountants, carpenters, futurists, physicians, salespeople, and just about anybody else you care to mention. Soon enough, you'll see that anyone can be creative in any job situation. It depends solely on you.

The amount of creative input that goes into your work can make the difference between meandering along uncertainly with only a mediocre future to look forward to, and confidently realizing your full potential. On a deeper, more personal level, creativity results in priceless rewards. No dollar value can be placed on self-satisfaction and pride in one's work. Suffice it to say that the amount of creativity you put into your work pays off in handsome dividends later on.

What, exactly, do we mean by on-the-job creativity? For now, think of creativity as the amount of imagination, productive input, and uniqueness you bring to your job.

What distinguishes the creative worker from everyone else?

- The creative worker is not a follower. By being creative in his work routines, he distinguishes himself from his fellow workers.
- He takes nothing for granted. Possessing an inquiring, information-seeking mind, he's seldom satisfied with the way things are.
- He seeks alternate paths ultimately leading to perfection.
- Before he's halfway through a task, he's already pondering the outcome or product, and what can be done to make it better.
- His mind is active; energy exudes from his pores.

What is the creative worker striving for? One thing is certain: it's a lot more than a job. If he is to realize his potential, he knows full well that a job is only a stepping-stone to building a career. A career, on the other hand, encompasses a broader reality and can be likened to a newly paved highway snaking its way from one place to another. It summons images of wide-open spaces, speed, and the freedom and curiosity to explore and experience life on a higher plane.

The creative worker envisions his career in multidimensions. From the onset, he is acutely aware of the fact that only *he* can chart his own course. He may be a tiny cog within an enormous organization, yet he knows that only *he* is responsible for his fate. Like everyone else, he has to conform to rules and regulations. Yet, if he is to step out of the crowd, he has to do things just a little bit differently. The challenge is hacking his way through the competitive underbrush and finding that alternate path leading to his goals.

The creative worker has the edge. He can bring something unique to his work. The challenge is getting in touch with his creativity, channeling it in the right direction, and going the distance. The creative worker has the power to distinguish himself, to stand out, to accomplish what his fellow workers cannot. The sky is the limit.

Can you be more creative in your work? Absolutely! Let me show you how.

Bob Weinstein

PART I

DISCOVERING YOUR CREATIVITY

CHAPTER 1
WHY YOU NEED
TO BE
CREATIVE
IN YOUR JOB

If properly channeled and harnessed, creativity can equal success. It can transform you from an ordinary worker with limited potential to one who's indispensable to your organization.

In order to advance, you must do more than what is required, or assigned. The challenge is finding out exactly what *more* and *better* means. Ultimately, it means doing things a little bit differently—taking mundane time-consuming tasks and finding faster, more efficient ways of doing them, looking for new approaches to traditional problems, searching for effective procedures that increase production and reduce overhead costs, developing new strategies, concepts, and ideas.

Quest for the Three Ps
(Power, Prestige, and Prosperity)

Early on, it's important to realize that creativity has its rewards. Beyond the personal satisfaction that results from coming up with something new, consider power, prestige, and prosperity, rewards that some idealists prefer to negate. They can range from a small promotion, a pat on the back, a paid all-inclusive vacation for you and family, to a Pulitzer or Nobel prize for writing an outstanding book or perfecting a serum to cure a life-threatening disease.

Keep these rewards in mind at all times. They make the game all the more exciting. Bear in mind that the rewards for creative efforts are relative, and not always fair. Society places different values on creative efforts, and, depending upon where you live and work, those rewards can vary tremendously. A machinist in Russia who designs a new method for producing machine tools may be singled out for an extraordinary accomplishment, and given a salary raise along with a modest promotion. On the other hand, an American worker who accomplishes the same feat may receive a salary increment to fit the deed and a pat on the back. In Russia, blue-collar creativity is applauded and encouraged, whereas in America it is treated merely as another on-the-job accomplishment worthy of a minor reward. Unfortunately, in the light of technological change, blue-collar work has been suffering from a poor image, whereas white-collar work is usually considered more valuable and more desirable.

Take the copywriter who writes an award-winning jingle and finds herself hurled to the uppermost ranks of her advertising agency. Her creative accomplishment is no less impressive than that of the machinist. It's just that in some industries the rewards of power, prestige, and prosperity are greater than in others.

There is nothing wrong with working toward a reward. It gives you the impetus and energy to work hard, and not stop until you accomplish your goal. All of us want different things, and it's important to get in touch with these needs early on. Chances are that you're probably more ambitious than you care to admit. You have great plans for yourself. You see yourself doing marvelous things, designing, planning, conceiving, and restructuring in order to come up with something that is entirely your own, an accomplishment that will be revered and praised by all who see it. But when all is said and done, the most meaningful reward will be simple acknowledgment. Few people will turn their back on a huge sum of money, yet money means different things to different people. Many research scientists, for example, couldn't care less about money (Albert Einstein, to cite one esteemed example). Many are content to earn enough money to support themselves and their families so they can devote themselves entirely to their work. However, the prospect of one day achieving recognition is a strong motivating force that few people would turn down.

Think about unleashing your creativity. Where would it lead? What would it bring you? What is it you want? Is it money, fame, notoriety, prestige, recognition? Or all of them? Don't be ashamed to say that your mouth waters when you mention power and money in the same breath. There is nothing wrong with wanting it all.

Hard work will *always* be rewarded. The productive worker is appreciated and applauded, but the creative worker reaps the biggest rewards. The worker who produces the most widgets will receive a sizable incentive reward at the end of the year, but the worker who designs an improved, tougher, longer-lasting widget might wind up owning the company one day. He can expect a promotion, recognition, more money, and a feeling of accomplishment from knowing he did something unique.

Don't think for a moment that entrepreneurial opportunities no longer exist. It's easy to absolve yourself of all responsibility for your fate by saying that sprawling multinational conglomerates are squelching all opportunities for potential millionaires. That couldn't be further from the truth. Multimillionaire J. Paul Getty maintained that anyone can be rich. In his book, *How to Be Rich*, he says: "The door to the American Millionaire's Club is not locked. Contrary to popular belief, it is still possible for the successful individual to make his million—and more. There will always be room for the man with energy and imagination, the man who can successfully implement new ideas into new products and services."

No truer words were ever spoken. And it's being done right now, by men and women who started with very little. Let's start with Steve Jobs, 28, cofounder of Apple Computer. A lot of people laughed when this college dropout insisted the home computer industry would one day be a billion-dollar industry. No one is laughing now. Jobs is worth well over $149 million.

While still in college, Frederick W. Smith came up with a unique idea for an airline. Instead of carrying people, Smith's planes carry packages of all sizes from city to city. The company, as you might have guessed, is Federal Express. Smith, at 39, is sitting on top of a spiraling empire.

Then there is Nolan Bushnell, a pioneer in the lucrative video game craze. His first invention was an electronic Ping-Pong called Pong, and it was heralded as the first successful coin-operated video game to capture the public's imagination. With this as the foundation for his empire, he went on to manufacture coin-operated games on a major scale by forming Atari, which was ultimately sold to Warner Communications for $28 million.

Is it still possible to rise from the technological dregs and launch yourself into position as a major power with wealth, possessions, power, status, and any other trappings you care to throw in? Absolutely. In fact, as the technological cold war intensifies, the need for hungry high-energy geniuses becomes more intense. As we said in the opening paragraphs, creativity has its rewards, not the least of which is money.

Let your imagination run *wild*. Go one step beyond the creative achievement and contemplate some of the ancillary rewards. The more you think about them, the more your imagination becomes fired and charged. If that isn't enough to whet your creative appetite, I don't know what is.

Harnessing Your Creativity

Surely, Thomas Edison and Leonardo da Vinci had preconceived notions as to where their dabblings might lead. They must have sensed that they were moving toward something special, unique, and uncommon. Something totally new that could revolutionize the world. Or maybe they weren't quite sure where their research would lead. Instead, they were driven by an incomprehensible energy that prodded them on and drove them to a point where recognition and discovery were the rewards, where creativity could be measured and applied.

Whether we're talking about inventors, scientists, artists, technicians, craftspeople, or executives, the creative person is the one most valued. He is the coveted jewel that's going to make the difference. He is the one who is going to put the company on the map, increase profits, reduce costs, create new products, end the war, reduce crime, and rid the world of disease. Governments, organizations, and corporations depend upon creative input; without it, progress cannot take place.

The history of mankind is an ongoing study of creativity in action. In a few hundred years we progressed from an agrarian to an industrial society, and then to a high-technology economy that is conquering new frontiers each year.

If it were not for man's creative energy, we'd still be hunting for our dinner with spears and rocks, and cooking it over open hearths. Our desire to grow, change, alter, and experiment has spawned every significant and insignificant innovation since the wheel.

And change is still taking place. Thanks to man's energy and talents, the future promises to be even more exciting than the present. Progress and change are functions of the creative process. Thwart creativity and progress falters. Curtail it for an indefinite period of time, and the world will surely stop rotating on its axis.

Being Creative in a Structured Environment

The truth of the matter is that most of us can't vent our creative impulses whenever we want to. Whenever a brilliant idea strikes us, we can't dart from the room into a special chamber and unleash our ideas in an inspired creative crescendo. It sounds romantic and exciting, but that's not the way the real world works.

The majority of us have jobs that we're expected to report to at a certain hour. We're required to put in a certain number of hours a day, and we're obligated to work five days a week before we're paid for our services. And within a given workday, we're expected to accomplish a certain amount of work and interact with other people. Like it or not, we have little control over the work routines that are presented to us. Yes, there is always room for creative variation, but for the most part we're expected to play the game according to the rules that have been established for us. Either that, or find another place to work.

The routines of the work setting are presented to us ready-made—our offices, fellow workers, lunch hours, coffee breaks, even our vacation allotments.

The challenge is *thriving* within that setting, finding that creative spark, dosing it with kerosene and magnesium so that a barn fire of ideas, concepts, and new thinking billows forth from predictable settings and routines. It happens every day, and it's that creative spark that turns jobs into careers, chores into obsessive passions. It can turn you about instantly. The energy that's bubbling inside you will be transferred to others, and before you know it, you're no longer just another worker but a prize, a find, someone who can do what others can't. In short, someone who has the creative input to improve and change his situation, thus benefiting yourself and the organization you work for.

How Employers Rate Your Creativity

Whether it's a formal or an informal procedure, employers are continually evaluating workers' performances to find out if they're working to creative potential. The reasons are obvious. The high-functioning creative worker is to be encouraged, rewarded, and given the necessary support so that he will continue to turn in impressive results. The low-functioning worker will either be told to mend his ways and improve his performance or be replaced by a more productive worker.

Let's take a look at some of the important characteristics that employers look for.

1. *Communication skills.* How well do you communicate your ideas? Can you organize your thoughts in order to be effective in speaking and writing?
2. *Group interaction.* How well do you work and interact in group situations?
3. *Judgment.* Do you have the ability to size up and judge difficult situations and problems?
4. *Involvement.* How involved are you in your work? Are you deeply, casually, or minimally involved?

5. *Excitement.* Are you turned on, stimulated, and fired by your work?
6. *Skills acquisition.* Do you have the necessary skills to perform your work well?
7. *Intelligence.* Do you have the ability to quickly digest directions and instructions?
8. *Confidence.* Do you have confidence in your talent, skills, or abilities?
9. *Self-starter.* Can you initiate projects and ideas, and then carry them out without supervision and direction?
10. *Responsibility.* Can you accept responsibility and not be flustered or intimidated by it?
11. *Initiative.* Once you understand what has to be done, do you take the initiative and try to solve problems on your own?
12. *Leadership.* Are you a leader or a follower? If your boss or supervisor is sick, can you take over and run the show?
13. *Energy level.* Do you maintain a consistently high energy level?
14. *Productivity.* Are you an average, above average, or extraordinary producer?
15. *Ability to take criticism.* Can you take and profit from constructive criticism?
16. *Goal directed.* Are you working toward specific goals?
17. *Attitude.* How would you describe your attitude toward your work—positive, negative, defeatist?

Where do you stand? Are you a creative asset to your organization? What are your strong and weak points? Before we move off to the Creative Motivation Scale in the next chapter, this is the time to start thinking about them.

CHAPTER 2
TEST YOUR
CREATIVITY

How creative are you? Let's find out. Tuck yourself into a quiet place and take the Creative Motivation Scale developed by Dr. E. Paul Torrance, a pioneer researcher in the field of creativity research. Once you've completed it, we'll show you how to score it.

Creative Motivation Scale

Indicate whether or not each of the statements below describes your attitudes and motivations. If the statement describes your attitudes or motivations, mark a "T" in the blank at the left of the statement. If it does not describe your attitudes or motivations, write an "F" in the blank.

_____ **1.** I think financial reward is the best incentive to good work.

_____ **2.** I am apt to pass up something I want to do when others feel that it isn't worth doing.

_____ **3.** I find it easier to identify flaws in the ideas of others than to think of other possibilities myself.

_____ **4.** It is hard for me to work intently on a problem for more than an hour or two at a stretch.

_____ **5.** I enjoy work in which I must keep trying out new approaches.

_____ **6.** I am fascinated by new ideas, whether or not they have practical value.

_____ **7.** My mind often gets so caught up in a new idea that I am almost unable to think of anything else.

_____ **8.** I thoroughly enjoy activity in which pure curiosity leads me from one thing to another.

_____ **9.** I enjoy trying out a hunch just to see what will happen.

_____ **10.** I never pay much attention to "wild" or "crack-pot" ideas.

_____ **11.** I enjoy experiences where I can't know what is going to happen.

_____ **12.** I feel upset when little things happen that I had not counted on.

_____ **13.** I sometimes lose myself in experimenting with an idea that may have no practical value.

_____ **14.** My interest is often caught up in ideas that may never lead to anything important.

_____ **15.** The presence of a group stimulates me to think of new solutions.

_____ **16.** When I get a new idea, I drop everything to try it out.

_____ **17.** I sometimes get so intent on a new idea that I fail to do the things I ought to be doing.

_____ **18.** I enjoy work in which I must change my course of action as I go along.

_____ **19.** I am inclined to be "lost to the world" when I get started on a new, original idea.

_____ **20.** I enjoy tackling a job that I know involves many as yet unknown difficulties.

———— **21.** I never feel really qualified when taking on a new job.

———— **22.** I have a feeling of excitement when an idea I am working on begins to jell.

———— **23.** I enjoy staying up all night when I'm doing something that interests me.

———— **24.** I frequently try things which do not occur to others to try.

———— **25.** I like to find ways of converting necessities to advantages.

———— **26.** I am willing to risk suffering for the sake of possible growth.

———— **27.** I see many problems to work on, much work to do.

———— **28.** I sometimes become childishly enthusiastic about an apparently simple thing.

———— **29.** I usually put a great deal of energy and zeal into my work.

———— **30.** I resist accepting the accustomed ways of doing things unless I can prove to my own satisfaction that it is the best way.

Finished? Now let's find out how well you did. Scoring is easy. Your score is the number of answers you marked "True." Take a look at the table below to find out how a one hundred percent creative person would have answered, then determine how creatively motivated you are by looking at the accompanying scoring chart.

Creative Motivation Scale Key

1. F	11. T	21. T
2. F	12. F	22. T
3. F	13. T	23. T
4. F	14. T	24. T
5. T	15. T	25. T
6. T	16. T	26. T
7. T	17. T	27. T
8. T	18. T	28. T
9. T	19. T	29. T
10. F	20. T	30. T

Interpretation of Scores for
Creative Motivation Scale

24 or higher: Exceptionally strong creative motivation, "hard to stop," not easily discouraged
21–23: Strong creative motivation
18–20: Above average in creative motivation
14–17: Average creative motivation
12–14: Below in creative motivation
11 or less: Weak creative motivation, hard to get motivated for creative thinking or expression

If you want to move up on the Creative Motivation Scale, work on developing some of the characteristics common to all creative people.

1. *Originality.* Creative people search for unique, special, or unusual qualities in a situation or person. The dare to hack through uncharted underbrush in order to explore new terrain. They have a burning passion to learn and discover.

Take the research scientist who is hellbent on advancing science's frontiers. He's like a bloodhound hot on the trail of an escaping varmint. He won't take defeat. If it takes all night, all week, or all year, he'll find the answer he's looking for. Like a magnesium-dosed torch, the creative spark burns hot and intense and won't be extinguished easily.

2. *Productivity.* An obvious correlation exists between productivity and creativity. Not all creative people are necessarily very productive, yet most productive people tend to be creative. A medical technician working for a large laboratory may be creative at different points of the year. Over a twelve-month period, for instance, he may make three significant contributions. Yet within that twelve-month period, he maintains a high degree of productivity, a lot higher than that of his fellow workers.

In the process of working and being productive, we often have the opportunity to express our creativity. The very repetitive movement of some chores, such as working on an assembly line, feeding a computer information, or building the foundation of a home, frees the mind and opens ourselves up to new possibilities and information. Through the motion of our routines, we discover that new opportunities and information are just beyond the horizon, if we alter our courses and do things just a bit differently.

3. *Adaptability*. Creative people can be compared to the wind and the elements. They're not static. They're always changing. They're adaptable, constantly searching for that which is off the beaten path. To harness their creative imaginations, they learn early on that they must achieve a harmony with their environment. Either that, or let their creative urges lie dormant and unfulfilled. Creative people fear compromise and mediocrity.

For many of us, there is comfort in doing the same things day in and day out, obstinately clinging to safe and confining routines. It's like crawling under the covers, closing the shutters, and remaining in the dark for the rest of your life. Without being aware of it, millions of people fall into this pattern day in and day out. Inevitably, they're suffocated by their routines. They become prisoners not of the institutions they work for, but, more subtly, of their own fears and weaknesses.

4. *Flexibility*. Adaptability implies a certain amount of flexibility. Whether we're talking about the nineteenth or the twenty-first century, change is a function of time. To cope with and ultimately to benefit from the millions of changes that take place within our lifetime, we must maintain a flexible attitude. In the course of our working life, we may have to alter our course in order to cope with unexpected variables.

One of the reasons life is so exciting is that it is unpredictable—at times almost incomprehensible. We can only *estimate* what lies ahead. Try as we may to steer ourselves in the right direction, often we have little choice but to resign ourselves to chance and fate.

5. *Analytical thinking*. The creative person develops an analytical, probing nature. Unconsciously, she breaks down concepts and ideas into their component parts. To understand something thoroughly, you have to see beyond its surface structure and expose its underside to see how it's put together. In nurturing something from conception to realization, a series of analytical maneuvers takes place automatically and spontaneously. If a concept is eventually going to see the light, all aspects of the project have to be meticulously researched and analyzed.

6. *Questioning nature*. The creative person instinctively questions everything. He accepts nothing at face value. If assumptions are to be made, they're based on facts. Before an idea is developed, he reaches into the past and asks important ques-

tions. Is there anything like it on the market? Who did research in the area? By questioning every phase of the creative process, potential flaws and problems are sidestepped and nothing is left to chance.

7. *Independent thinking.* The creative thinker has to maintain a degree of independence. In order to come up with something new, he has to step out from the crowd and view it from a distance. While he has to know who his predecessors were, what kind of research is taking place, or if there is anything remotely like his idea on the market, he has to keep his distance in order to remain objective. Above all, he has to be an independent thinker. In order to create something new, he has to be a critical observer. His eyes are cameras and his ears are tape recorders. Information is collected, analyzed, and stored in order that he can render an independent judgment. The creative person learns the importance of being independent and self-sufficient. If he is to realize his abilities and accomplish his goals, he must remain his own person, clearly distinguishable from the crowd.

8. *Sensitivity.* Creative people have sensitive natures. The more creative you are, the more sensitive you are to the world around you. You're touched by things that leave others cold. You see shades and hues where others see only one-dimensional colors. Your sensitivity to both your inner and outer world gives you a special edge. It allows you to see things others don't and to feel and experience sensations that spark your creativity and motivate you to produce that which is out of the ordinary. The creator's sensitive soul and spirit allow him to explore, delve, and make new discoveries. It is through the process of discovery that new creations are born, and the world eventually changes because of it.

9. *Unconventionality.* Every creative person you can think of has an unconventional core to his nature. But don't be deceived by outward appearances. If you're under the impression that creative types are society's oddballs, sporting beards, mustaches, long hair, earrings, torn jeans, and faded T-shirts, you're unable to recognize the creative people around you. More typically, the real creators are the ones you'd least suspect. They're living within society and working toward making a contribution that will benefit themselves and the world around them. While they're independent, sensitive, and unconventional, they're very much a part of the world. What makes them different is not the clothes on their backs, or their hair styles, but the way they think.

10. *Courage.* Finally, it takes a good deal of courage to realize your creative potential. We don't ordinarily associate courage and creativity, but they're intimately related. I'm not talking about the kind of courage it takes to go ten rounds with a mean-looking middleweight, or the courage needed to trek off to war, not knowing whether you'll ever come back alive. That's one kind of courage. It takes another kind of courage to create something, and have enough confidence in it to try and convince others of its uniqueness and value. As any individual daring to try something different will tell you, it can be an uphill struggle all the way. You may be a budding Edison, or a genius entrepreneur the likes of Bernard Baruch, but don't be naive and expect your ideas to be greeted with open arms. Sometimes they are, more likely not. We tend to be skeptical about that which we don't understand. It's at this telling crossroads where no one wants to listen and rejections are coming fast and furious that courage is called for. Courage means believing in yourself and your ideas enough to hurdle all barriers blocking you. As you'll see later on, stamina, self-assurance, and a cast-iron will are often needed.

In conclusion, the creative person who is working to capacity and realizing her potential is also in harmony with herself. Above all else, she is constantly replenishing herself by gorging her creative appetite with new information and ideas. Soon enough, you'll be amazed at how effortlessly everything will fall into place and all the creativity characteristics described above will apply to you.

CHAPTER 3
WHAT IS
CREATIVITY?

Whether we realize it or not, we all have creative energy bubbling within us. It's just a question of discovering it, and allowing it to express itself. Prevent the creative energy from flowing and you remain stuck, immobilized. You'll remain in the same humdrum job until you're retired or fired, whichever comes first. Worse yet, you'll experience a more horrible fate. You'll suffer the debilitating pangs of inertia and apathy. Life will hold little meaning, challenge, or fervor.

Creative energy is a life force. It is that which distinguishes you from every other human being on earth. It is that which is yours, separate, complete, and untouchable.

Successfully channeling your creative energy will help you

stand out and achieve your goals. If you were a millionaire a hundred times over, I daresay you'd be unfulfilled if you weren't harnessing your creativity. It's your most valuable asset. For these reasons, we should do everything in our power to stimulate and cultivate our creativity.

In the Introduction, imagination, productive input, and uniqueness described creativity. They all apply. But let's go on and try to get a better grasp of the word. The dictionary provides some straightforward and surprisingly simple definitions. On *creation*, it says, "The act of making, inventing, or producing." For *creative*, "productive," "having the quality of something created rather than imitated." And for *creator*, "One that creates usually by bringing something new or original into being." The synonym for creator is simply "maker."

When you look at the word clearly, you see that there is nothing complicated about it. Yet you can apply it in a trillion different ways and still not exhaust all the possibilities before you.

When I think of creativity I think of *birth*—birth of a child, animal, idea, or concept. What happens during the mysterious process of giving birth to a child? All of a sudden, something new enters the world. What could be more exciting? Out of a woman's body comes a brand new life. Who will the child look like, what sex will it be, what kind of person will it be are questions every parent ponders. The birth of a child is both simple and complex, and never forgotten. Despite technology, we'll *never* top it.

Yet the same wondrous process can be applied to the creation or birth of an idea. Creativity, regardless of form or type, involves a process. The process can be altered, and adapted to varying situations and stimuli, yet the process is essentially the same, regardless of your goal. As we said in the Introduction, creativity isn't a word reserved exclusively for painters, composers, and writers. Everyone—from child to senior citizen—can be creative in his work. The principles we're going to outline for being more creative on your job can easily be applied to other areas of your life.

Let's take a closer look at the creative process, and outline a few of the steps that make it up. They can be applied to anything from developing a new way of manufacturing a product, marketing a program designed to introduce a new concept, and introducing a system for getting work done faster, to writing a novel or painting a landscape.

The process is broken down into six alterable parts. There are no hard and fast rules governing the creative process. The steps outlined below are to be used as a guide. For some, the process may include only three steps; for others, six. Let's look at the six-step process.

Creative Process

1. Idea/problem
2. Evaluation
3. Development
4. Completion/test phase
5. Revision
6. Completed, workable product

---

1. *Idea/problem.* Start with a statement, problem, or idea—such as designing a new light bulb, creating a better marketing program for a product, proving the world is flat, building a replacement product, writing a novel about the Vietnam war.

The idea/problem stage is nothing more than a statement of purpose, or your goal. Since this is the first stage of the creative process, begin with an idea that is simply stated. Your task may be monumental, but your statement of the problem must be simple. For instance, the task at hand is proving that Columbus did not in fact discover America and that it was actually an Irish naval officer named Timmy O'Hara. As farfetched as it sounds, your problem is clearly stated, and your goal is to prove that Timmy O'Hara discovered America. In one crisp statement, your problem or idea is laid out for you.

Keep your problem short, sweet, and understandable. Once the problem is before you, your mission is obvious.

2. *Evaluation.* This is the research stage. You have your idea, now what? Do you go off half-cocked and start making plans to

activate your idea, prove your premise, or put your product into production? Do you build a house without knowing if the land can support it, what materials you'll need, and whether you can afford the expense?

I hope not. Regardless of what you're attempting, it could be a foolish, time consuming, not to mention costly, mistake. At this point, all you have is a plan, concept, or idea more fragile than an eggshell. Before you can go further, the following questions have to be answered:

a. Is there anything like it on the market? Has a competing inventor, scientist, businessperson, craftsperson, come up with the same idea?
b. What was done in the past? Has there been research in an allied field?
c. What will it cost to develop the product? Can you afford it?
d. What materials are needed?
e. How long will it take?

3. *Development.* Now we're moving. We've evaluated the idea to the point where we're ready to produce and launch it. The development phase is the action phase of the creative process. The wheels start moving, the manufacturing process begins, plans are activated.

4. *Completion/test phase.* Product is finished, idea is developed. Now what? Another probing question. Will product, idea, concept, plan do what it's supposed to do? Yes, I know, you're raring to get it to the public so that everyone can benefit from it and you can see returns on your hard work. Not so fast. You've come this far, you don't want to risk making mistakes. Just as a car is road-tested over grueling conditions, your idea has to be similarly tested.

5. *Revision.* If your product or idea came through the test phase with flying colors, you can bypass the revision stage and go right to the final phase, and launch your product. But if problems were found, this is the time to patch the trouble spots.

6. *Completed, workable product.* You've done a fantastic job. Give yourself a congratulatory pat on the back, knock wood, and think positively. It's time to see how the public reacts to it.

An even simpler way to approach the creative process is to break it down into three all-purpose steps:

Creative Process

1. Encounter/observation
2. Engagement
3. Development/completion

This is merely a variation on the above-mentioned longer process, which is a common creative problem-solving technique.

In the *encounter/observation* phase, you face the problem, or challenge, head on. Again, it can be anything from executing a difficult painting, or summing up a company's product in fifteen seconds, to finding a faster way to mass-produce a machine tool. Once the problem is understood, you tackle it. This is the important *engagement* stage, where you're consumed by the product, determined to find the answer, produce the definitive product, or come up with the mind-blowing slogan that will launch it. During the second stage, emotions run high and you, as creator, become passionately involved with the mission at hand—taking it from the idea stage, encountering (or observing) it, and finally taking it through a series of stages until it is completed.

Even within this simpler three-stage creative process, there is often a time lapse between the encounter and engagement phases. You may have a brilliant idea that you don't know what to do with. You'll carry it around with you for weeks, months, sometimes years, trying to work the problem through and *develop* it so that it will finally see the light of day. This is the gestation period, where the idea simmers and nurtures before it can be fully developed (more on this later).

Sometimes the idea is forgotten and dies, and the creative process never gets beyond the conception stage. Compare the process to the hatching of an egg. It takes a while before a baby chick can fend for itself and leave its mother. Some chicks never make it. They're neither strong enough nor aggressive enough, and they're destined to die prematurely. So it is with ideas that never go anywhere, and never reach the development phase.

Finally, look upon the creative process as an emerging circle. The birth of the idea is the beginning of the circle, maybe one-quarter of it. The encounter and engagement phases comprise one-half the circle, and the final phase where idea, concept, or product finally sees the light of day is the remaining fifty percent of the circle.

1. Encounter/observation

2. Engagement

3. Development/completion

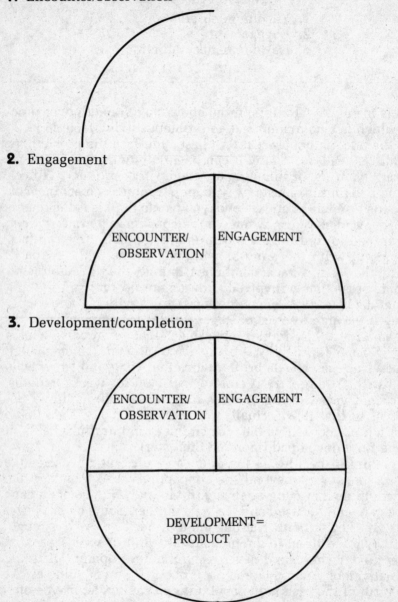

Think of the creative process in terms of some illustrative examples and then apply it to yourself. Imagine what Thomas Edison felt like when he dreamed up the electric light bulb or phonograph; Alexander Graham Bell when he conceived the telephone; the Wright Brothers, the airplane; Jonas Salk, a vaccine to prevent polio; Tolstoy, when he finished long passages of the mammoth saga *War and Peace*. Beyond these supercreators, there are lesser-known individuals whose creations had a profound effect upon the way we live. Take the individuals who invented the can opener, Saran Wrap, flip-top bottle, disposable bottle, retortable pouch, and so on. Each creation had an effect upon our lives, not to mention the feelings of self-satisfaction they gave their creators.

What about yourself? Think about your own creativity and the effect it has on yourself and others. In school, for instance, you might have had the foresight to develop a unique idea into a major treatise that was largely responsible for your graduating at the top of your class. The suggestion you made to your supervisor for speeding up the assembly line, which resulted in a finer product and increased output, was a creative act responsible for promoting you from line worker to assistant supervisor. Or the system you presented to the chief accountant at your firm proved to be a brilliantly thought-out cost-saving measure, which eventually improved profit margins by twenty-five percent.

Now you can see that the creative process is essentially a variation on a common theme. The result, the creation, may be earth shattering and revolutionary, it may benefit millions, or just yourself. Regardless of its dimensions, it is an accomplishment to be proud of.

Once you appreciate the creative process, it's important to understand the extent of your creative efforts. As we said above, there is creativity that is unique only to the individual and creativity that affects others. You may, for example, create something that has already been on the market for years. Since you didn't realize that somebody else had already conceived and developed it, your accomplishment is no less significant. And since your creation came second, the only recognition you'll enjoy is the feeling of accomplishment that comes from knowing you did it. However, if you're a pioneer, and your creation affects millions, you'll enjoy widespread recognition for your efforts.

No matter how you look at it, creativity is anything but a straightforward process. It can involve anything from simple problem solving to achieving something unique and outstanding.

CHAPTER 4
HOW YOU CAN
APPLY
CREATIVITY
IN ANY JOB

As we said, anyone can be creative. Still doubtful, are you? Let's run through some random occupations, and you'll see how creativity can make the difference.

Clothing buyer. The creative buyer avoids ordinary run-of-the-mill clothing and concentrates on unusual, futuristic creations that will captivate a consumer's imagination. She develops an innovative approach.

Architect. Instead of designing houses and office buildings the way they've always been designed, he designs new, daring structures that put his work in a special category.

Salesperson. There are millions of salespeople earning very decent livings. However, the creative salesperson is not content merely to earn an average income. He formulates new selling strategies and experiments with different selling approaches. As a result, he covers more ground, makes more and bigger sales, earns more money, and stands an excellent chance of being promoted to management's ranks.

Secretaries. In the midst of their daily routines—taking dictation, typing, filing, and answering phones—they discover a new way of billing, an improved selling tactic, the bare concept of an exciting public relations campaign, and so on. How often does it happen? More often than you realize. Many ambitious secretaries use their creativity to hurdle themselves into executive positions.

Advertising copywriter. There is no telling how far a creative copywriter can go. The one who comes up with a winning slogan, or a high-powered radio and TV campaign, will reap the biggest rewards. Creativity runs high in the advertising business, but copywriters who churn out consistently creative copy earn the biggest salaries and last the longest.

Electrocardiograph (EKG) technician. The creative EKG technician takes nothing for granted. Instead of performing routine procedures that were taught to her in school, she questions everything, looks for flaws in traditional methods. More likely than not, her inquisitive, creative, information-seeking mind will lead her to better, more accurate, and faster procedures.

Library technician. The creative library technician is more than a support worker who assists librarians. This person is intent on bettering his position, and improving his lot in life. At night he attends college working for a degree in library science; during the workday he finds new ways to get his work done faster so he can have extra time to study and prepare for class.

Optometrist. Not content to examine eyes and write prescriptions for glasses, in his spare time he diligently works on a new design for an inexpensive, safe contact lens; or on a lighter, cheaper frame made from an experimental metal; or on improving poor vision through controlled nutritional programs.

Geologist. A creative geologist employed by a major oil company does more than spend her time searching for oil. In her free time she researches the feasibility of using geothermal energy to generate electricity. If she accomplishes her goal, millions of people will profit from the discovery.

Police officer. The creative police officer wants to be far more than a cop on the beat for his entire career. He uses creative energy to better his position. Four nights a week he attends a nearby college and works toward his bachelor's degree. With a bachelor's degree in political science, he stands a better chance of being promoted to detective. From there, he plans on working his way up to captain and possibly beyond. Creativity along with hard work, and the sky is the limit.

These are only a few examples. Mention one thousand jobs and I'll show you how you can be creative at each one of them. Creativity can take place on many different fronts. It can be used to improve your position; get you a raise; help you do better work; revamp procedures; conceive, design, or build something from scratch—on and on. In sum, there is no end to what creativity can do for you.

Let's get more specific and isolate the creative aspects of our job. From there we can arrive at an approximate creativity quotient and discuss the differences between direct and peripheral creativity.

The creativity quotient is the amount of creativity that goes into your work, and the difference between direct and peripheral creativity concerns your relationship to the creative process. *Direct creativity* is when you are the sole creator, whereas in *peripheral creativity* two or more people are working together. It's important to add that some jobs are inherently more creative than others. As we said earlier, you can be creative in any job situation, but in some cases it's more of a challenge.

Take the assembly line worker employed by a computer parts company. There isn't too much room for creativity here. This person is saddled with one routinized task after the next, minimal thinking is required, and he is little more than a human machine. His job is to keep up with his machines and meet his production quota.

What is his creativity quotient? To be generous, anything from two to five percent, and if he is creative, he'll be employing direct creativity. Nevertheless, our blue-collar assembly line worker can be creative if he is determined and inventive enough to change his situation. He can alter his situation by finding a better, faster, or more efficient way to produce the same product. At that point he is no longer an ordinary line worker, but someone who is looking for a way out. His only escape route from the tedium of the assembly line is through successfully harnessing his creative energy. It may take work and thought, and consume most of his coffee and lunch breaks, but the rewards speak for themselves.

An attorney, on the other hand, has more opportunity to be creative. Since he works by himself and with others (especially if he is part of a law firm), he may be employing both direct and peripheral creativity. And depending upon the type of law the attorney practices, creativity may account for a significant part of his job. A corporate attorney, for instance, may employ more peripheral creativity, whereas a criminal attorney relies on direct creativity in formulating effective courtroom strategies.

And the creativity quotient? Considering all the variables, an attorney's creativity quotient may run anywhere from thirty to sixty percent.

What about the attorney's secretary? Is there creativity involved in her work? More than you realize. If she is aggressive, and determined to better her condition, she may be employing anywhere from a twenty-five to a fifty percent creativity quotient by designing strategies that better her boss's position within the firm, by creating faster, more efficient systems for getting work done, or possibly by playing a subtle but no less persuasive role in the corporate decision-making process. A secretary's role is anything but dull and routine these days. As office automation revolutionizes the contemporary office, secretaries will be free from the tedium of traditional office chores to do more demanding, challenging, and, yes, creative tasks.

Take the high school math teacher. There are teachers, and there are teachers. Some teachers play the game according to the bureaucratic rule book, while others invest a good deal of creativity in their work by daring to do things a little bit differently. They veer from the norm, go beyond traditional curriculums, inculcate new information, and excite their students by imparting their own enthusiasm and zest for learning. Now we have a teacher who is a cut above the norm, someone who employs direct creativity, with a creativity quotient ranging from forty to sixty percent. A creative teacher can go on to become a master educator. She can break new ground by writing textbooks and eventually becoming prominent in her field.

To change gears slightly, a trade magazine editor has the opportunity to employ an even higher creativity quotient, if she chooses to tap her abilities. Don't make the mistake of misreading the road signs. Just because she is a writer/editor, don't overestimate her creative input until you know what she is putting into her work. If she is just getting by doing what she is told, turning out machine stories, and rewriting press releases, her creativity may be a very average forty to fifty percent, which is nothing to get excited about, considering the nature of her work. Yet, if she's generating stories, coming up with original ideas, expanding the scope of her magazine and even dreaming up new advertising strategies, she's operating on a much higher creativity plane. Now she's functioning at a creativity quotient ranging between sixty and seventy-five percent, employing direct creativity when she is working by herself and peripheral creativity when she is brainstorming ideas with colleagues.

Can jewelry retailers be creative? You bet they can. Again, it depends on what kind of retailer we're talking about. If we're focusing on a shrewd businessperson who is constantly on the lookout for unusual jewelry and makes it a point to deal with talented craftspeople, a great deal of creativity goes into her work. If that person is also a top-flight salesperson, creativity plays a major part in her retail operation.

Our jewelry retailer can demonstrate a creativity quotient ranging between thirty and sixty percent, depending upon the factors discussed above.

The jewelry designer employs a still higher creativity quotient. If it's a one-person operation, it involves direct creativity all the way. Since a high level of creativity goes into costing, estimating, analyzing trends, and designing jewelry, the creativity quotient can go as high as eighty-five to ninety percent, depending upon the imagination and originality that go into the designer's conceptions.

A pharmaceutical salesperson also has to use both direct and peripheral creativity in his work. If he's planning strategy with his supervisor, he's peripherally creative, but when he is in the field on his own, it's direct creativity. Nevertheless, talented, successful salespeople have to employ a great deal of creativity in their work. A hotshot salesperson has to be part psychologist, part businessperson, along with knowing his product from stem to stern. Prior to making that final sales pitch that could make him just a little bit richer, he has to plan his moves as a chess player would when competing against a tough opponent. What type of strategy should he employ, hard sell, soft sell, laid back, or a flip almost casual approach? I've watched crackerjack salespeople operate, and the best of them are so adept at molding their personalities to the situations at hand, that they probably could have made it as character actors. In sum, the pharmaceutical salesperson may demonstrate a creativity quotient ranging between forty and seventy percent.

Finally, a free-lance technical writer, working alone in his own disciplined self-styled environment, employs only direct creativity. And since his work involves a great deal of research, the creativity quotient is not as high as that of a fiction writer churning out gothic novels. Depending upon the amount of original writing he does on any given day, his creativity quotient can range from a low of forty percent to as high as seventy-five and eighty percent. Whereas a gothic novelist, for instance, may employ anywhere from a ninety to ninety-five percent creativity quotient when he is in his stride.

This gives you a brief sampling of how different workers employ creativity on their jobs. As you can see, it varies from job to job, and from person to person. Think about your own situation and try to determine the amount of creativity used on your job. Use the guide below to help you compute your creativity quotient.

Computing Your Creativity Quotient

Your creativity quotient is only a subjective estimate, so it's difficult to come up with a figure that's one hundred percent accurate. Be honest, though, and try to compute an approximate number that describes your creative input.

Within an eight-hour day, how much of your time centers around using direct or peripheral creativity? On a piece of paper break out a typical workday, hour by hour, to find out exactly how your time is spent. Next to each hour list the approximate amount of time you're being creative. When you've added up the amount of time spent in creative pursuits, you're ready to compute your creativity quotient by dividing that number by the total number of hours worked.

Use the examples below as your guide:

Workday—8 hours
Creative input—2 hours $\quad \frac{2}{8} = .25$ or 25% Creativity Quotient

Workday—8 hours
Creative input—4 hours $\quad \frac{4}{8} = .50$ or 50% Creativity Quotient

Workday—8 hours
Creative input—5 hours $\frac{5}{8}$ = .65 or 65% Creativity Quotient

Workday—8 hours
Creative input—6 hours $\frac{6}{8}$ = .75 or 75% Creativity Quotient

For the above illustrations, we used the standard eight-hour day. However, you may work only seven or seven and a half hours, or maybe as much as eight and a half or nine hours, giving you a different creativity quotient.

Now that we have some idea about the amount of creativity used on our jobs, let's find ways to overcome barriers to creativity.

CHAPTER 5
OVERCOMING
BARRIERS
TO
CREATIVITY

Before we go further, it's only fair to outline common barriers you may encounter. It's important not only to know the characteristics of the creative person, but also to be aware of the obstacles blocking creativity's free expression. Let's take a look at some of these common roadblocks and show you how to overcome them.

Lack of self-confidence. Many of us don't have enough confidence in our abilities to put our creative talents to the test. The creative conditions may be perfect, yet we're blocked by our own inadequacies. We're bright enough, we're highly trained and competent, yet we don't dare trek off on our own. Why? Psychologists trace the roots of the problem all the way back to childhood. As we said in Chapter Two ("Test Your Creativity"), creativity is often discouraged when we're very young. Every time we tried to go it alone and construct, invent, or do something that was different, we were told to do it as it always has been done. When our imaginations ran wild and we tried to construct the house of the future out of blocks, our mothers told us to build a conventional block-style house with fireplace, front yard, and furniture neatly in place. No wonder many of us are petrified when it comes to venturing forth and conceiving something on our own. Before we start, we're defeated. Just as the urge to do something surfaces, it's squelched by a little voice in the back of our head that says, "Why bother! You won't succeed. Save your energy. It's already been done before. Why don't you stick to the conventional way of doing things."

It can be likened to telling a young child not to attempt walking. "Don't do it!" says a powerful authoritative voice. "You'll hurt yourself. Crawl instead, it's safer." Fearing for her life and terrified of the unknown, the child crawls until someone comes along and deprograms her and convinces her there is nothing to fear.

Lack of self-confidence coupled with an inability to appreciate your self-worth can *cripple* you into immobility. Because of it, millions of people never tap their creative core and as a result never reach their full potential.

Overcoming a lack of self-confidence may take a little time, but it can be done. It involves a two-stage process: *confrontation* and *rebuilding*. In the confrontation stage, you're going to unearth the factors that contributed to your lack of self-confidence. You say you don't know what they are? Be patient, and you'll find answers. Before we can begin to patch the troublespots, you have to know why you're feeling that way and why you lack confidence in your talents and abilities. I am going to show you how to isolate the negative tapes that are still running in your head, preventing you from moving forward and accomplishing your goals. You're not only going to stop those tapes, you're going to destroy them once and for all, and replace them with new, positive, affirmative ones.

Think back to when you were a teenager, or go back even further if you can, and find three important occasions where you were riddled with self-doubt and lack of self-confidence and write them down on a piece of paper. It could have been a speech you had to make in front of hundreds of people, an interview, or a performance in a school play. Next to each one, list circumstances or memories surrounding those events and answer the following questions:

- What were you feeling at the time?
- What kind of support were you given by friends and relatives?
- Why is it you didn't think you could pull it off? What exactly was blocking you?
- How did you handle it? Were you successful, or did you fail?
- What factors contributed to either success or failure?

If you learned something from this exercise, you may be motivated to go back even further in time. The further you go, the more you learn. Initially, we're reluctant to turn back the clock and look at our past closely. But once you pry open one creaking door, others begin to gently swing on their rusty hinges. You'd be amazed how far back you can go. Some people have uncovered incidents and events when they were two years old. Seems extraordinary, but it can be done.

In the rebuilding phase, your task is to embrace and tackle any problem or creative challenge that comes your way. You're not to back off as you did in the past. You've found and destroyed the negatives tapes—the cancer has been exorcised—now it's time to repair and heal the wounds. The only way to combat a lack of self-confidence is by dealing with it directly.

Imagine that a unique opportunity arises and you have to convince others concerning a great idea. This time you're going to confront the situation, deal with it, and accomplish your goal. Naturally, you're frightened. It's to be expected. But you can do it. Before tackling the situation, ask yourself these questions:

1. Do I have the talent to pull it off?
2. Do I have the necessary knowledge to carry it through to completion?
3. Do I have the experience to convince others?

Naturally, the answer will be yes to all of the above. One more question, *Do I still lack self-confidence?* I doubt if you'll totally eradicate all of those old feelings, but I bet you have far more control over the situation than you did before.

Boredom and apathy. In the process of creation, excitement and enthusiasm are generated spontaneously. They provide a protective halo of support around the creative act. What can be more exciting than devising, planning, originating something that was never done before? On the other hand, if working conditions are unfavorable, and you're unhappy or bored with your job, it's practically impossible to rev up the creative wheels. Everything around you is working against that end. What can be done? You have three choices:

1. You can try and alter your situation so that boredom and apathy are replaced with excitement and enthusiasm.
2. You can change your attitude.
3. You can find another place to work.

Achieving any of these ends may take time and work. You have to decide which one makes the most sense.

Let's say you work for a large corporation and your talents are all but buried because you work with low-functioning, barely motivated employees. Since there is an escape hatch available to you, why consider moving to another company? Using tact and diplomacy, you can present the problem to a supervisor or vice president and if he values your services, he'll make sure you're transferred to a department made up of high-energy, aggressive workers like yourself.

Or the problem may be rectified simply by changing your attitude. Instead of letting other workers drag you down to their unimpressive production quotas, you resolve to let nothing stand in your way. A quick turnabout in attitude and you're wheeling and dealing like a seasoned pro, impervious to those around you, intent on climbing to the uppermost reaches of the corporate hierarchy.

However, if you worked for a small company offering little opportunity to change or better your position, you're left no alternative but to bail out and find another job. Needless to say, in this competitive job market, don't hand in your resignation until you've landed a job that meets your specifications.

Before taking action, study your options. If you're not working to capacity and fully exploiting your creative potential, it's time to do something about it. Consider all the alternatives, weigh pros and cons of contrasting strategies, and take action.

Lack of support, group interference, and criticism. Rare is the person who works in total isolation. Most of us weave support systems around ourselves. Even the writer who works by himself in a small office miles from noise and distractions builds some kind of sturdy girder of support that encourages him to work and be productive. Within an organization, a worker has to know that he is part of a team and that the team is behind him. In this kind of environment, accomplishments are shared and encouraged. A personal creative victory is also a victory for the organization.

Remove this sturdy internal support system and the individual flounders and loses grounding. Where he once had definite organizational roots and ties, he's now cut off and barely subsists in a non-nurturing environment.

Just as bad as having no support is encountering group interference. Every time you try to test a new idea on your supervisor, you're shot down before you can explain the entire concept. Or in the process of brainstorming an original idea your colleagues rally against you, frustrating and thwarting all creative attempts. In an airless environment like this, it's impossible to achieve satisfaction and realize your potential.

Before we outline a couple of suggestions, it's important to understand human nature and organizations. It's unrealistic to expect to glide through life without encountering barriers in your path. Within your company, you can count on playing subtle power games. Individuals and even groups of allied workers may try and prevent you from achieving your ends. If there are five candidates being considered for a pending vice presidency, and you are one of them, you'd best arm yourself for battle. Whether it's corporate or government politics, it's survival of the fittest all the way.

How do you cope with lack of support and group interference? The easy way is to throw in the towel and find another place to work before things get hot. I'd consider that option only as a last resort. Instead of crumbling before the opposition, consider this strategy:

- Make friends and establish loyalty bonds.
- Create your own support groups.

In large companies, this is done all the time. In any well-established organization, the new person is inevitably confronted with cliques and support networks. Don't try to be a one-person song-and-dance team and go it alone. You'll regret it later on. It's not going to happen immediately, but in time you'll find co-workers who think and feel the way you do, whose ideas and goals parallel yours. Befriend them, take strength from them, use them as weapons to gain ground. Soon enough, your support group will be powerful and influential enough to rally against group interference coming from unknown sectors of your company.

In the final analysis, corporate maneuvering amounts to a series of power plays. The individual who knows how to use and wield power, form power groups, and use them as a battering ram to convince others, will go the furthest.

Think about your own organization and ponder the following questions:

- Are you a lone individual fighting VPs and colleagues who are thwarting your progress? If so, what can be done about it?
- What kind of a support network can you form? Who are the sympathetic workers who think and feel the way you do?
- What has to be done to change the status quo so you can see your ideas and plans come to fruition?

And what about criticism? As much as you'd like immediate acceptance of an idea or proposal, it's an unreasonable expectation. No matter how brilliant, innovative, or earth-shattering it is, there is bound to be criticism to overcome. That's the way the game is played.

Let's look at a couple of classic cases. The Wright Brothers' crude double-wing flying contraption was greeted with anything but enthusiasm. Critics, colleagues, and the public at large thought the two brothers had gone clear off their rockers. Imagine the comments. "It's unnatural." "Man wasn't meant to fly." "You've got to be kidding with that pile of paper, wood, and wire. It's never going to get off the ground." Crude it was, but it worked, and look how far we've come. Now we have the Concorde that can fly from New York to London in less than four hours. And who's to say what will replace the Concorde in another decade or so?

Or what about the reaction to color television and stereophonic sound? When companies began introducing their color televisions to the market, the public wasn't impressed. They thought they were ridiculously overpriced and a gimmick. Most people weren't convinced that color television could actually do what it was touted to do and that it was any better than black-and-white reception. Now most homes in this country have at least one color television, and many have two or three sets.

When introduced, stereophonic sound was also not greeted with open arms. At the time, the consensus was that it was a gimmick concocted by big record companies to sell more equipment and records. Monaural high fidelity was the prevailing fad, and few people could understand why it was necessary to go to the trouble of having two distinct sound channels when one sufficed.

You know the rest of this story. Now you can hardly find a teen or adult who doesn't own a stereo set, and it won't be long before stereo radios are standard equipment in new automobiles. As for those old cumbersome monaural sets, practically the only place you'll find them is in antique stores and flea markets.

An entire book could be devoted to noteworthy inventions that were initially greeted with skepticism or criticism. For some, the criticism was so vociferous that acceptance was postponed several years before the public decided to view them objectively.

How should you handle criticism? Before proposing an idea, concept, plan, or system, mentally prepare yourself for obstacles beforehand. Strategy:

- Play devil's advocate. Before you outline that winning idea, put yourself in your colleague's shoes and draw up a list of ten criticisms of your idea. Maybe even extend it to a list of twenty criticisms if you can. Leave no stone unturned. Try to anticipate every obstacle before you. It's analogous to planning a battle maneuver. The field general about to launch an all-out frontal attack on his enemy plans every move of his campaign down to the most minute details. He can't afford to take any chances. Every possible contingency is accounted for. A mistake could result in the loss of lives and costly equipment.
- Have ready answers, formulas, and solutions to every criticism. Just as the attorney prepares his case for trial, make sure your case is airtight. Believing in it is not enough. Make sure you know how to defend it as well. If you're lucky, your colleagues will see your idea for what it's worth and accept it immediately. Nevertheless, you still have to go in armed and ready to do battle. Why take chances if you don't have to?

Bad habits. Bad habits can be unlearned, yet if nothing is done about them, they can stifle creativity in the bud. Instead of proceeding logically and thoroughly, you'll look for shortcuts, trying to cut corners to save time and effort. This is a poor tactic to take and the results are sure to be second rate. Good work habits, on the other hand, that include care and precision in executing your work, are essential for good results.

How do you overcome a bad habit? First, isolate the bad habit you want to work on and look at it closely. Answer the following questions:

- What is it you're doing wrong?
- Are you racing ahead without considering the results?
- Are you sloppy, impulsive, careless?
- Do you rely on others when you should be puzzling things out for yourself?

With a little knowledge on your side, take your bad habit and put it under a high-powered microscope in order to look at it further. Take a piece of paper, fold it down the middle, and list all facets of your bad habit on one side; then, on the other side, list what has to be done to correct each facet.

Imagine you're a slipshod report writer who reluctantly has to turn in a number of well-written reports each month. Instead of carefully outlining what has to go into each report, step by step, before writing it, you bound ahead and scribble the first thoughts that pop into your head. The result is a wordy, poorly prepared report.

But once you look at your mistakes, using the above method, you'll see where you went wrong and begin to correct the bad habit. It's not easy pulling in the reins and proceeding logically when you want to get something over with as quickly as possible. With concentration, thought, and a great deal of patience, you can do it.

The Inspiration Myth

Hollywood has had a field day depicting inspired, possessed creators. The most memorable are as mad as hatters. One, say, is going about his work in a whirlwind of activity. As you might expect, all of a sudden a brilliant idea strikes him while walking down the street and he has all he can do to get home in time to get it all down on paper. Better yet, the crazed, dedicated, hirsute scientist awakens in the middle of the night as an inspirational wave points him to the hypothesis he's been waiting weeks to uncover.

It's time to clear the air. Some people think inspiration and creativity go together like a hand in a snugly fitting glove. If you're waiting for that special moment when an inspirational tornado will lift you off the ground and propel you at supersonic speeds toward exalted creative heights, you're in for a rude awakening.

If creativity were to depend solely on inspiration, few innovations would be produced in any given year. This is not to say that inspiration is not important. It certainly can be. Great things have happened at inspired moments, yet it's important to understand that just as many great things have happened in the course of going about one's daily routines.

Must you be *inspired* to be creative? Again, the answer is no. Waiting to be inspired can be the greatest cop-out for not doing any work at all. A jewelry maker friend is a case in point. This wildly imaginative artist says he can work only when inspired. When he works, which is not very often, he produces strikingly original creations. The pity is that the man's talent is wasted since his output is so small he can barely make a living. His waiting for inspirational flashes is a marvelous rationalization for not producing. The upshot is that many of his competitors who don't possess his talent have overtaken him. Their output is consistent, they have excellent distribution channels, and they enjoy good reputations, whereas stores are reluctant to deal with my friend on a regular basis because of his erratic work habits. Can you blame them?

The true creators in any profession, be they scientists, mathematicians, businesspeople, carpenters, craftspeople, painters, writers, or technicians, work constantly and, in the process of working, inspiration often takes root by itself. For most creative people, inspiration comes through the process of working on an hourly, day-to-day basis.

We've spoken a little about inspiration, but what is it exactly? When I asked a talented advertising copywriter who has a couple of award-winning ads to his name to explain the part inspiration plays in his creative psyche, he laughed and said, "If I waited to be inspired before turning out a piece of copy, I'd be a very poor and unhappy person. Truthfully, I'd be out of a job and my family and I would have to stop eating for an indefinite amount of time."

Not that inspiration doesn't play a part in his work. "It's marvelous when I am inspired," he goes on. "Everyone experiences inspiration differently. I describe it as a feeling of great energy where out of nowhere I suddenly find direction and guidance. Prior to that moment, I am trying all kinds of paths to find the right one. I'm looking for an approach or concept that will sell the product or thing I'm writing about. When I'm inspired, suddenly I know, or think I know, where I'm going."

He added that very often an inspired moment leads down a blind alley. "The burst of energy, which I call inspiration, doesn't always lead to anything fruitful. Sometimes it does, but very often I have to go back and rewrite and redefine what I have done hours or days before. So inspiration is not always the foundation for creativity of a higher order."

In sum, this copywriter finds he has little choice but to sweat over much of what he does. "Sometimes pulling good ideas out of my head is like extracting impacted wisdom teeth from my jaw." Nevertheless, he adds that the product is more often than not first rate, making all the hard work worthwhile. So inspiration is not always the panacea for excellent results.

In a conversation with Christian Zervos, Picasso frankly discussed his work habits: "The picture is not thought out and determined beforehand, rather while it is being made it follows the mobility of thought." Picasso talked at great length about his work and his views on the process of creation. Not once did he use the word "inspiration."

An energetic marketing strategist for a large California-based market research organization describes his inspired moments as waves of ideas that overtake him at odd moments. "Usually, I am relaxed when I'm inspired," he begins. "I'll be driving home on the Santa Monica freeway with the radio playing softly and a couple of great ideas will come to me. Or I'll be sitting at a bar with a couple of friends chatting and sipping a martini when all kinds of great ideas hit me. Some of those ideas are quite good and many of them, to my surprise, have already been done or are less than mediocre. I guess the peripheral conditions are so pleasant when these inspired ideas come to me, I tend to make more of them than they really are."

He went on to say that the strongest, most consistent ideas do not come from random inspired moments, but through the process of working consistently.

All things considered, it's important to see inspiration for what it is. Yes, it can play a significant part in the creative process. But don't make the mistake of sitting back and waiting for it to happen. However, when inspiration does strike, don't let it slip through your fingers. Morning, noon, or middle of the night, get in touch with it, experience it, feel it, break it down into its component parts. Milk it for everything it's worth. Consider the following suggestions:

- Take detailed notes. Record everything that comes to mind. Don't rely on memory.
- What conditions prompted the inspired moment (what were you doing at the time? Where were you? Who was with you at the time? What were you thinking about?)?

Why all the fuss? If you're in touch with what was going on at the time, you may be able to duplicate those same conditions again. Think about it. How marvelous it would be if we could set the stage and inspire ourselves on a whim! It makes your mouth water when you consider what you can accomplish during those simulated inspired moments. Yet, be practical and realize that we can only control our working conditions to a certain extent.

Stress

Some of us think stress came in with the twentieth century. We think of technology, the frantic pace, uncertainties of contemporary life, keeping up, our futures, on and on. True enough, all of the above factors are stress producing. Yet the twentieth century has no lock and key on stress. Yes, the word has become popular, but also bear in mind it's been around for centuries. And as long as man occupies this planet, there will be stress.

What exactly do we mean by stress? Broadly speaking, it can be a chemical, physical, emotional, or psychological reaction to change. Using that all-encompassing definiton as a frame of reference, it's not hard to see that we've always had to cope with stress. What has changed is the degree and amount of stress that the average person has to cope with. Since life is a lot more complicated than it was at the turn of the century, it stands to reason that it is also a lot more stressful. Nevertheless, stress is a part of life and, more important, necessary for survival. What we fail to appreciate is that stress, if understood and channeled, can augment the creative process.

In *The Natural Way to Stress Control*, Dr. Sidney Lecker says that no one is born with the ability to control stress properly. Says Lecker: "The experience I have had as a psychiatrist in private practice and also in my work with corporate executives at the STRESSCONTROL Center in New York has convinced me that the difference between people who succumb to stress and those who effectively control it lies in the strategies employed when encountering a taxing situation. Time after time, when cases are reviewed and analyzed, a similar pattern emerges."

Some of us react well to stressful situations; others do not. In other words, we react either positively or negatively to the stress-producing changes in our lives.

Let's take the negative reactions first. Imagine you're a precision tool designer and you've been given a large order to fill within three days. You realize you've bitten off more than you can chew, but times are hard, you need the money, and naturally you agree to do it. Ordinarily, the job would take better than a week. What you didn't plan on coping with is the accompanying stress. Undertaking the project was more than you bargained for. The more you think about the pending deadline, the more uptight and frightened you become. Negative thoughts race through your head: *What if I don't finish the order in time? My credibility will be ruined. I won't be able to make my mortgage payments.* To relieve your anxiety, you pop a tranquilizer and, without realizing it, you're up to two packs of cigarettes a day.

Judging by this person's reaction to stress, you can see how a negative stress reaction can be destructive over a long period of time. Everyone's negative reaction is different, yet all of them are ultimately debilitating and counterproductive. Common stress reactions include overeating, drinking, chain smoking, pill popping, and plain old worrying. All they do is remove the initial symptoms of stress and delay the inevitable—confronting the stressful situation.

I'm sure you can compile a list of at least ten stress-producing incidents you encounter practically every day. Maybe they begin with the daily mad dash to make the seven-forty-five train to the city. After that, they break down to a series of confrontations with clients, staff, bosses, and family.

Be realistic. You'll never be able to eradicate all the stress-producing incidents in your life. But you can effectively cope with them and not crumble when they present themselves.

How do you deal with a stressful situation? Through positive interaction. We've already outlined some negative reactions to stress. Now let's take a look at the flip side. Let's go back to our precision tool designer for a second, and see what a positive stress reaction looks like. Instead of rushing for tranquilizers and cigarettes and working himself into an anxious state, he mobilizes himself for action. Naturally, he's nervous and tense, and he's aware of the adrenaline pumping through his body. But he applies the brakes of reason and uses a little mind control before expending needless energy. Instead of bolting into action, he thinks about the project before him. What has to be done? What materials do I need? What's the quickest, most effective way to get the job done? Before beginning, he focuses on the cause and outlines a plan to allay the stress as quickly as possible. Instead of channeling that energy into a negative response (reaching for alcohol, pills, food, etc.), he uses it constructively to attack the problem at hand.

Once solutions and a plan of action are crystallized, he begins working. Now stress is used for a positive end. The energy produced by the stressful situation is harnessed, thus eliminating the causes of stress.

Now you can see how stress can be a positive factor in channeling creative energy. Stress energizes and propels you, creating the initial momentum to meet the problem head-on. When this happens, ideas are structured and formulated, concepts developed and crystallized. In essence, creativity takes place under optimum conditions.

To review, here's strategy for coping with stress-producing situations:

1. *Identify situation.*
2. *List stress-related fears.* For instance, you're uptight about not making a deadline; being prepared for a presentation; meeting out-of-town clients; convincing a major investor.
3. *Formulate ten-point plan.* In ten or more steps, list what has

to be done, in order of importance, to complete the task at hand. Once you're systematically working to realize your goal, and accomplish the job at hand, stress will be greatly reduced and subsequently eliminated.

Fear

Just as stress can energize you, fear can cripple you and bring you to a dead stop. First, let's put fear into perspective. We're all afraid of something. I know of no one who doesn't have at least one fear, no matter how innocuous. As a wise man once said, "Only a fool is not afraid of something." And chances are you'll never overcome all your fears.

You can go through your entire life with a fear of water, height, and small spaces. But if you fear people, aspects of your work environment, new things, or success or failure, your creativity will be stifled and your progress will be slowed considerably.

Merely telling yourself there is nothing to be afraid of is as useless as telling a soldier not to be afraid of war. Unfortunately, fears cannot be turned off as you would a faucet. As difficult as it is, we must get in touch with them and deal with them, one by one, consciously and with sincere effort. A fear, whether rational or irrational, is real and threatening. It's understandable that the process of getting in touch with it and dealing with it can be painful and frustrating.

To make the process a little simpler, we've outlined three essential steps that will help you overcome fear.

1. *Confront your fears.* What is it you're afraid of? Look at your fears critically and without embarrassment. Instead of thinking about them, say them out loud to yourself. No one is listening. Things take on a whole new dimension when they're said, as opposed to read or thought. The spoken word is often more powerful and penetrating than the written word. Try to grab hold of your fear and confront it. Bounce it from one end of your being to the other, sit on it, wallow in it, experience it.

2. *Analyze your fear.* Once in touch with your fear, play analyst and try to get to the root of it. You've admitted your fear, now find out where it came from. It's not easy, but see if you can

unearth some of those dusty cobwebs in your mind. Just as you unearthed the causes for your lack of self-confidence, you'll again have to go back to your childhood to find out where your fear began. You say you're stumped and can't find the origin of your fear. Look at it another way. Ask yourself the question, *What is it about a particular situation that upsets or frightens me?* If it's fear of meeting people, communicating, and establishing rapport, what is it about it all that scares you, or terrifies you?

Or jot down on a piece of paper all the things that terrify you about certain situations. You may find that doors begin to open. For the first time, you may confront the causes of your fear. Bits and pieces of understanding surface and you begin to learn something about yourself. Flashes of childhood experiences start to rocket through your consciousness and the origin of a once-buried fear is now excavated to a conscious state. Slowly, things begin to fall in place. Characters assume their rightful positions on stage, and you begin to see things in a new, penetrating light.

It may take time and a good deal of probing self-analysis, but it's possible to get to the heart of your fear. Some of us can do it ourselves, others need the help of skilled therapists to guide them through the dark byways of their subconscious minds. Whatever method you use, don't give up.

3. *Visualize success.* Once you've isolated and analyzed your fear, it's time to work with it so you can eventually overcome it. An effective way is to envision, or visualize, success.

In the visualization process (which will be discussed in more detail later on), we're going to harness our imaginations. What will it take to eradicate your fear? Chances are it's not one, but several things. On a piece of paper create a simple chart listing five components of your fear. Next to each component, list a necessary condition that will wipe it out.

Imagine that you're fearful of meeting new people and face an important sales meeting with a potential client. The very thought of the meeting paralyzes you with fear. You're so uptight, you can hardly fire your creative resources to prepare a hard-hitting sales presentation that will snare the account. What do you do? Walking into the meeting trembling and stuttering is not going to get you very far. Days before the meeting is the time to prepare for the confrontation. Instead of letting your fear get the better of you, take the encounter apart piece by piece as shown in the chart below:

Fear of Meeting New People	Alternate Condition Eradicating Fear
1. Sales presentation will be flawed and not geared to the market.	**1.** Absurd! You're a specialist when it comes to preparing this kind of sales presentation. No one knows the market and the client's needs better than you. What's more, you have the support of every VP in your company.
2. They won't like me.	**2.** You're an accomplished pro with twenty years in the business; how can they not like and respect you?
3. I am inadequately prepared.	**3.** Would you dare walk into a meeting inadequately prepared? You'll do everything in your power to prepare for the meeting.
4. What if there is a hostile reaction?	**4.** They want to cement the relationship as much as you do. Don't you realize they need you as much as you need them?
5. I will stumble while making sales presentation.	**5.** So what if you do? No one is perfect. If you stumble over a phrase, back up and take it from the top. It can happen to anyone.

All you're doing is playing a little game with yourself. In the visualization process described, we're taking the fear-producing situation and working it through, thus taking what used to be a negative reaction and making it positive.

Let's face it, anyone walking into a new situation is going to feel somewhat awkward and nervous, especially an important meeting with a lot riding on it. Top executives and politicians often admit to being uptight before an important speech. Even professional actors admit to being nervous before going on stage. It's a normal reaction.

Our fears have rational bases to them, yet they often manifest themselves in irrational ways. In our fear of meeting new people, people are not seen as other human beings. Instead, they take on monstrous proportions. They're not 5 feet 8 or 6 feet 1, but 10 feet and 15 feet tall. They're dangerous, threatening, they have powers you don't have. But is any of the above true? You know the answer. Switch on the reality button once again. They too have bills to pay and wives, lovers, or children to support.

Prior to the meeting, play the scene as you'd like to see it played over and over in your mind. See the people, hear the conversation, and take it through its various stages. Chances are it won't go exactly as you envisioned it, but you'll be surprised how close it comes to the real thing.

Let's say you're afraid of criticism. The thought of people criticizing your work, or your dazzling new creative idea, makes you turn crimson with embarrassment. You view criticism as an attack. Your idea, work, intelligence, and very being is put on the chopping block. When it happens, you feel like curling up in a corner, hiding your head, or apologizing profusely. Instead of defending yourself, and hurling back solid arguments supporting your idea, you assume you're wrong.

Instead of crumbling in the face of criticism, let's look at the situation closely using the chart mentioned earlier.

Fear of Criticism	Alternate Condition Eradicating Criticism
1. Criticism is viewed as an attack.	**1.** How can it possibly be an attack? All someone is doing is expressing an alternate opinion. Have you ever criticized or found fault with another person's idea?
2. I doubt myself and my idea.	**2.** Be realistic. You've spent months, maybe years, working on the project. How could you doubt yourself? You know your subject thoroughly. You're an expert. Think of all the knowledge you've acquired.

3. How do I defend myself?

3. Not with your fists, but with well-substantiated arguments driving home the point that your idea is valid and you know exactly what you're doing. You know how to proceed, you just weren't prepared for this moment.

Again, we've turned the fear-producing situation around and looked at it in a new light.

Visualizing success implies viewing situations, people, and things objectively, not subjectively. When your fears get the better of you, subjective feelings take over and control the situation.

But you can deal with fear. First, you must want to come to terms with it. Then you have to look at your situation rationally rather than emotionally. After that, you simply take on the challenge of working toward and achieving your goal.

Now that we've overcome some of the obstacles, let's gather the bricks, cement, and steel beams, and lay the groundwork for creativity.

CHAPTER 6 LAYING THE GROUNDWORK FOR CREATIVITY

For many of us, getting in touch with our creativity first involves a process of unlearning many of the rules and tenets taught to us as children. Before we can be creative, we have to know that it's okay to dabble, to make broad sweeping strokes as we did when children, before we can refine those lines to come up with something new, different, and maybe even better than that which exists.

It's never too late to learn. As adults, we can learn to incorporate creativity into our work and personal lives. It can make the difference. The creative person is continually searching for new ways of doing things—shortcuts, improvements, refinements. Often, it means contemplating the impossible in order to make something happen.

Now that we've learned something about the subject of creativity, let's find out what has to be done to get in touch with our own creativity.

Get in Touch with Yourself and Your Skills

The creative person is in touch with himself and is able to see himself clearly. To function like a well-oiled machine, he's learned to see himself objectively.

Rare is the person who is a jack-of-all-trades and master of all of them. There are things you do extremely well, just as there are areas where you're only competent. Know what they are. Let's start with social skills, and move to job skills.

How do you see yourself socially? Are you extroverted or introverted? If you had a choice of working quietly at your desk all day long undisturbed by others or working in the field meeting new clients and drumming up business, which would you prefer? You may do both well, but which do you enjoy more? Few people can achieve or create the perfect job situation for themselves, but it's important to get as close to it as you possibly can. Some of us thrive in a group setting, while others can work at optimal efficiency only when left to their own devices. And then there are those who need a balanced environment that consists of interactive relationships along with working quietly by oneself. Where do you fit in? Take a close look at your job situation and see if it's meeting your needs. Is there enough people contact, or do you need more time for yourself in order to develop ideas that have been simmering in the back of your mind?

Let's go on to *skills*. Do you have the right skills and training for your job? To be fully creative, you need the tools of your trade and the right training. An auto mechanic, for instance, no matter how talented he is, can't fix your car unless he has the right tools. Without tools, he's practically useless. On the other hand, an apprentice mechanic may have every conceivable tool at his disposal, but if he lacks talent and competence, he'll never amount to very much. The worker who is fully trained can function at optimal efficiency and is apt to be more innovative and creative on his job than the worker who has only a minimal amount of experience. If you want to be the very best, most creative, and highest-paid worker in your particular field, you must know your job from stem to stern, know it better than anyone else. You must be accomplished, confident, and highly skilled. More exactly, you must be a master craftsperson at whatever you do. The fully qualified, high-energy worker is more apt to be creative and productive than the unmotivated worker who hasn't invested the same amount of training in his career. The more effort and sweat you invest in your career, the more determined you'll be to succeed and reap hefty rewards. And along with that determination goes the incentive to do things just a little bit differently and a little bit better than your colleagues. The seeds for being more creative at your work have already been planted.

Just as you need the right social skills for your job, you also need the right technical, vocational, and professional skills. I can't stress enough how competitive the present job market is. At no other time in history has skills acquisition been so important. We're living in a technological marketplace that is changing as you read this page. Many commonplace skills we take for granted today will not be around in another decade.

In the past, you could have spent three to five years learning a trade or profession and never had to think about going back to school once you completed your training. This is no longer true today. The theme of the future is continuous retraining, or reeducation, throughout our working lives. This applies to everyone, no matter what you do.

Needless to say, individuals involved in high-tech businesses such as telecommunications, data processing, and many of the hot engineering fields will have to stay current with state-of-the-art developments. Companies like IBM, Honeywell, Data General, and others provide their engineers, consultants, and technical staffs with continuous refresher courses. Many insist that their engineers, scientists, and technical staffs attend weekly or monthly seminars so they can keep abreast of developments in the field.

In the health-care professions, there are new developments every year, new life-saving techniques and machines, along with new professions and technologies to accompany them. Even the small independent businessperson must stay current with his field so that competition doesn't overtake him. It may mean constantly improving his product and services, and possibly purchasing a small computer to facilitate inventory control and speed up end-of-month billing procedures.

Technology has permeated the very fabric of our lives, affecting the way we live, work, and play. Built into our high-speed technological marketplace is change. If we hope to make a creative contribution, earn a good living, and realize our potential, we have little choice but to stay current and monitor the times. Either that or be drowned in a sea of insurmountable technological breakthroughs. In this day and age, there is nothing more humbling than being overshadowed by a computer that can outproduce and outlive you.

To prime oneself for what lies ahead, the savvy creative worker has to do both a personality and skills tune-up to make sure he is in step with the market. From time to time, ask yourself the following questions: Do I have the necessary technical and social skills for my job? How has my field changed over the past few years? What changes are taking place right now? What changes can I look forward to in the future?

To be creative in this tough, demanding marketplace, you have to be more than in step with the technology of the day, you have to be a giant step ahead of it.

TO SUM UP

1. Get in touch with your strong and weak (personal) selling points.
2. Determine if you have the right skills and training for your job. If not, do something about it.
3. Take a close look at your job situation and see if it's meeting your needs. Is there enough people contact, or do you need more time for yourself in order to develop ideas that have been simmering in the back of your mind?
4. Being the very best means knowing your job from stem to stern, knowing it better than anyone else. It means being accomplished, confident, and highly skilled—a master craftsperson at whatever you do.
5. To be creative in this highly volatile marketplace, you have to keep pace with technological developments and have one foot firmly planted in the future. Otherwise, you could be overtaken by a machine that is smarter and more productive than yourself.

Like What You Do

To be successful and creative at your work, it is important that you like—or, better yet, love—what you do. Not that it's impossible to be creative at a job you're superficially interested in. It can be done, it's just so much harder. Why start off with a built-in handicap? Considering today's tough job market, you're wise to find a career that fires your imagination, one that you'll be deeply involved in until retirement.

We're not saying you won't do some job hopping in the course of your career. It's to be expected. Unusual is the worker who takes a job and stays at it until retirement. Working conditions change, your fellow workers change, or the company takes off in new directions. Most important, you change, which necessitates emptying your desk and moving on to greener pastures. It's safe to say the average worker will change jobs a few times throughout his career, each move hopefully strengthening and bettering his situation and providing him with the diversified experience and knowledge necessary for creativity.

There are no clearly stated givens for being more creative in your work and achieving success in your field. But what you can do is at least steer yourself in the right direction. As early as you can, find that special career that will turn you on for the rest of your working life. In some respects, it's more important than finding a suitable mate. In these troubled, freewheeling times, it's easier getting married and divorced than it is changing jobs. If you've got the resources, you can divorce one woman and marry another, all within a twenty-four-hour period. But without a good deal of meticulous planning, try walking out of one job and into another. Unless you planned the move months in advance, you're in for some surprises. In these hard times, it's quite common to be out of work for anywhere between three to six months, sometimes longer. So know the characteristics of the job market before you embark on a campaign. Try to avoid being in the tense and uncertain situation of having to change career direction midstream. No matter how good you are, that's a tough move.

As one industrial psychologist said, "We're on a high-speed treadmill and the competition to bolt through the ranks and achieve a top flight job and salary to match give far too many people ulcers and heart attacks way before their years." In the past, it wasn't uncommon to decide upon a career when you were in your sophomore year of college. Today, you're wise if you have your sights set on a career in your sophomore year of high school. In the future, who's to say parents won't start teaching their children career basics as soon as they learn how to walk and talk. Sounds a little forbidding, but without a career that excites and motivates you, you'll never achieve a fulfilled and happy life, much less a creative one.

No matter how you view the situation, long-range career planning pays off. Regardless of the field, the creative worker who's functioning at maximum efficiency is passionate about his work. His world revolves around his job.

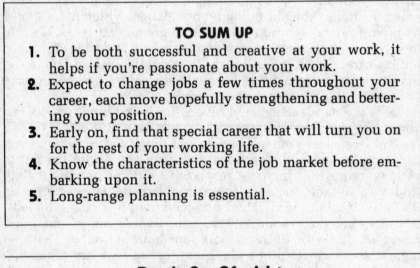

TO SUM UP

1. To be both successful and creative at your work, it helps if you're passionate about your work.
2. Expect to change jobs a few times throughout your career, each move hopefully strengthening and bettering your position.
3. Early on, find that special career that will turn you on for the rest of your working life.
4. Know the characteristics of the job market before embarking upon it.
5. Long-range planning is essential.

Don't Be Afraid to Express Your Individuality

All of us are born with a unique creative spark. Initially, the flame is small, but nevertheless, it's strong and ready to be fired and intensified to a point where it can melt steel.

We pass through three broad phases, and the duration of each phase depends upon the individual and the unique characteristics of each situation. Let's take a close look at each phase.

1. *High creativity.* We arrive in a world without rules. Everything is new and we're encouraged to express our uniqueness.

We eat when we want, we play when we want, and we get to sleep as much as we want. What a life! In our waking hours we dazzle ourselves with our discoveries. With each discovery our creative instincts are fired for the first time. Each day brings something new. One day we uncover a hand and fingers, the next day another hand, more fingers, legs, face—till we've found our entire bodies. Now the fun begins. Once we connect our extremities and realize we're a whole human being and that all our parts somehow mysteriously work together, we begin the exciting and unending process of creative exploration.

First, the tools of creation (hands, fingers, eyes, ears) have to be discovered before creation can take place. Then we can dabble, build, draw and for the first time watch our hands create new things, faces, strange-looking animals, free-form sculpture. Anything we want. Creativity first takes place on an elemental level. Each primitive creative act leads to a more refined and defined product.

Present a child with a piece of paper and a felt-tip pen and before you know it she's drawing broad sweeping lines and circles that may not look like much to you and me, but to the child a work of art is unfolding. It may be nothing more than random doodling, yet the child is testing and exploring an unknown world. If left alone with enough pens and paper, new drawings emerge, each one a refinement and improvement over the preceding one. In time, the child learns to alter and temper her movements so that concrete forms emerge from random scribblings. In other words, the child learns to be creative. While she may be doing something every other child has done since the beginning of time, the behavior is, nevertheless, unique to that child.

From nothing at all, new things are created that provide a sense of joy, fulfillment, and excitement. We're thrilled with our new-found talents, we're delighted and mystified by the process of creativity, and, most important, we want to develop it further. As we grow, new and more startling discoveries are made every day.

The next time you have the opportunity, observe a child as she discovers her world. Once a discovery is made, creative exploration takes place. The discovery is meticulously explored before it is taken apart, reconstructed, or used as the foundation for building something different. Not only is it an exalting experience for the child, it's also a rewarding one for the viewer, because the observer gets to see something each child experiences in her own unique way. The creative process is taking place on a simpler plane, yet it's the foundation for greater discoveries later on.

2. *Conformity.* Sociologists use fancy words like acculturation and socialization to describe this phase. We're not going to go into detail on either word. Let's just say *acculturation* takes place when the individual acquires the culture of her society and *socialization* is the process where the individual learns the behavior patterns and rules appropriate to that culture. In short, learning on a broader scale takes place.

As the child gets older, she is entrusted to others and begins to learn the dos and don'ts of a conformist world. She spends time in play groups and nursery school, exposing her to structured play patterns and regimented games. Protective limits are placed on her that are part of the socialization process. She moves from activities that are unstructured (early days spent in crib or playpen exploring world by herself) to activities that are structured and orderly.

Soon enough, the child learns to follow rules. First encounter with school is a case in point, setting the pattern for the rest of her life. The day is carved into orderly time frames with rules, order, and discipline built into the system. So begins a pattern that will follow this individual through life. After grammar school and high school, there is college and possibly graduate school. Then into the work world, which insists upon a great deal of conformity.

Where does it leave us? Should we abandon all rules and regulations and let our children discover life for themselves? Not at all. That would pose more problems—uppermost is anarchy, a far more frightening state of affairs. Clearly, children, as well as adults, need rules and regulations in order to function in the real world.

Yet with all the rules, standards, codes, and restrictions, we have an unconscious need to create something that's entirely our own, to express our uniqueness, our individuality. It can take any number of forms. In school, it may express itself in the form of a special project that is very different from anything done before; a hobby that taps hidden talents; a home-styled system of studying that is faster and more efficient than the official one; or the desire to be an expert in a certain subject, thus giving creative leverage for acceptance into a top college.

You've heard the expression, "Rules are made to be broken."

For the creative person, the phrase would read, "Rules are to be expanded, shaped, elaborated upon, changed, made better, improved." For the creative person, conformity serves as the incentive and motivating base for creative activity of a higher order.

To put the three stages into definable time frames, the first stage ends when the child starts school, and the second stage terminates when our acculturated, socialized individual is educated and trained, and ready to make her mark on the real world.
3. *Achievement/creativity*. Here's where the fun begins. We're starting out on an exciting, often mysterious journey into the work world and we're not quite sure where it's going to lead us. Whether we're aware of it or not, we're entering the most creative period of our lives. We're like a racehorse at the starting gate, raring to go, foaming at the mouth, listening for the crack of the gun signaling the start of the race.

However, not everyone is going to run that race. Those in touch with their creative abilities are champing at the bit, ready to dart off down the track. Those who are not are little more than observers. Instead of joining the race and tapping their creative resources, they've opted to hide behind their routines, recording little progress.

In this period of achievement/creativity, you have the opportunity to break out and accomplish great things. You're an adult, you've had sufficient training, and you're ready to assert your individuality.

Look at it this way. Two workers approach a restrictive rule in different ways. The bored, apathetic worker sees no way around it. For this worker, rules are designed to keep line workers in tow so that they perform their work and maintain production quotas. Rules are to be obeyed and there is no beating the system. The creatively motivated worker, on the other hand, views a restrictive rule differently. He refuses to be done in by it, and will not let it cramp his style or inhibit his creativity. The more restrictive it is, the harder he works to find a way around it, or a better way to do the same chore. He's determined to find an alternate path. His goal is to redefine or amend the rule so that it gives him the latitude and freedom to express his creativity and individuality and harness his imaginative powers. Despite restrictive rules, he's driven to change the system, or at least to redefine it, so that he can make a creative contribution, thus bettering his position and possibly improving the system in the process.

It's not going to be so easy. As we said, the routines of the world are givens. They're not going to go away. What's more, by this time you know how necessary they are. Whether it's a nine-to-five work world, or possibly a flextime arrangement where you work three nights and two days, you'll still have to contend with routines, schedules, and rules. The challenge for you is finding that alternate path, breaking out of the routines, redefining the routines, or simply being creative within those routines. It's up to you to find a solution.

View your situation realistically. The routines, structures, and disciplines of your job are not going to go away. You're not going to walk into work one day and be delighted to find an absence of corporate routines and tiresome memorandums demanding your immediate attention. All the middle management heads that monitor your work are not going to be sick at the same time so that you can have free rein over the department to test the ideas you thought about late at night.

Nevertheless, employers, relatives, and loved ones encourage you to express your creativity, develop it to the point where all your great ideas are realized. Easier said than done. You find you don't have the time, the environment isn't stimulating enough, you're afraid to stick your neck out with a new idea, you don't have the equipment you need, and so on. There are a million and one excuses for not pursuing and developing that great idea. With all of the above working against you, you certainly have the opportunity to take the easy way out and quit before anyone expects anything more of you. It's a safe, comfortable, and anxiety-free solution. Or you can take the bull by the horns, muster your forces, rev up your creative machinery, and determine not to stop until your idea is realized. In other words, resolve not to let anyone or anything prevent you from expressing your individuality, and realizing your creative potential.

Set Specific Career Goals

Once in touch with your uniqueness, set realistic goals. Having realizable goals removes the clutter from your mind and gives you a direction that allows and encourages you to be creative.

In this tough competitive job market, precise, targeted moves are called for. If you're not quite sure where you're going, you

TO SUM UP

1. In the course of living, we pass through three broad phases: high creativity, conformity, achievement/creativity. The duration of each phase depends upon the individual and the unique characteristics of each situation.

2. The first stage ends when the child starts school, and the second stage terminates when the socialized individual is educated and trained, and ready to make her mark in the real world.

3. During the high-creativity stage, the child is allowed and encouraged to express her creativity freely on her own terms without being impeded by external rules and pressures.

4. During the conformity stage, the child learns to follow rules and guidelines. But despite the rules imposed by parents, school officials, and institutions, we have an unconscious need to create something that's entirely our own. It takes different forms in terms of hobbies, special projects, or the drive to be an outstanding or unusual student.

5. During the achievement/creativity stage, we strive to assert our uniqueness, express our individuality, and fine-tune our creative powers, despite restrictive rules and routines. In this final adult phase, we can, if we dedicate ourselves to the task, achieve greatness in our respective fields.

can almost count on winding up in the wrong place. Let neither fate nor the wind assume responsibility for your career. Only you can do it. And, as we said in the previous section, meticulous planning is essential. Planning implies setting logical goals. In the past, goal setting wasn't a major strategic maneuver. Today, the distance from point A to point B can involve 25 intermediate steps, all of which have to be conquered to realize your goal. So it's important from the outset to have a clear idea of where you're headed.

Prepare Goal Statement

Most of us have a long-term goal in mind. Somewhere down the road we see ourselves snaring that big job, being promoted to division manager, director, vice president, district manager, research scientist, supervisor, engineer, or maybe even president of a major Fortune 500 company. All worthy goals.

While it's all well and good to have a solid long-term goal in mind, it doesn't take on lifelike proportions until it's clearly stated. Hence, the necessity of writing a goal statement. A goal statement is nothing more than a phrase that crisply describes your ultimate career goal. The key words to keep in mind when writing your goal statement are *concise* and *accurate*.

Write down your goal statement and compare it to the sample ones below:

1. To be a well-paid auto mechanic
2. To be a successful accountant working for a large firm
3. To be an aggressive trial attorney
4. To be a pediatric psychiatrist working at Sloan-Kettering Institute
5. To be a jet pilot capable of flying the SST Concorde
6. To be president of a large bank

Look at each one critically. Which ones are concise, complete statements that tell you all you need to know about a particular goal? If you said (4) and (5), you're on target. What about the other ones? Not enough information is included in (1), (2), (3), and (6). "To be a well-paid auto mechanic" doesn't tell us enough. A job recruiter wants to know what kind of auto mechanic, and possibly where that mechanic wants to work. Does he want to concentrate on foreign, American, or sports cars. Does he want to work for a large dealership or a two- or three-person shop?

"To be a successful accountant working for a large firm" is also a vague goal statement. What's missing? What kind of accountant? Corporate, tax, small business? Does he want to work for a small or a large firm?

"To be an aggressive trial attorney" tells us little. It's nice to know this person is aggressive, but what kind of law does he intend to practice? Trial attorneys come in different varieties.

Does he want to practice criminal, civil, negligence, or corporate law?

The same rationale applies to wanting "to be president of a large bank." What kind of bank are we talking about? Commercial, savings, special category? Even the use of the word "large" raises still more questions. What does he consider large?

"To be a pediatric psychiatrist working at Sloan-Kettering Institute" tells us a great deal. In ten words we know exactly what he wants. He doesn't want to be a general psychiatrist, but a pediatric psychiatrist practicing in one of the finest hospitals in the country. The same goes for our jet pilot. This person wants something special. He's not content to man the controls of an ordinary commercial jet. He wants to fly the SST Concorde, the fastest commercial airliner in the sky.

As you see, clarity is important. A good goal statement doesn't take many words, but those words have to say a great deal. How does your goal statement shape up?

Match Your Goals and Abilities

Before you do some long-range planning, ask yourself the following questions:

1. Do I have the right credentials and skills to realize my long-term goal?
2. Do I have the right temperament?
3. Am I willing to put in the time and effort required to realize that goal?

If your answer is yes to all of the above, you're ready to proceed.

Before you set out on that long trek to your goal, find out if you have what it takes. Let's say your goal is to be a broadcaster working for a cable television station. An exciting career with a tremendous amount of growth potential. However, the only experience you have is working for a commercial television station as an administrative assistant. Since you have no experience in broadcasting, making the career change will not be easy. It will take a good deal of planning, along with some calculated strategic career moves that will take you out of one setting and into the setting of your choice.

Possibly after giving the above-mentioned career change a good deal of thought, you may come to the conclusion that it's not worth the trouble. After weighing the pros and cons and the problems involved in trying to break into broadcasting with no prior experience in the field, you may decide that it makes more sense to reevaluate your goals and go off in another direction.

From the beginning there has to be a compatible fit between your abilities and goals. You don't open an appliance repair shop unless you're a first-rate mechanic; attempt to become a systems analyst unless you have a solid working knowledge of computers; or think of becoming an astronaut if you're deathly afraid of heights. The examples are somewhat exaggerated, but they drive home the necessity of having the right skills and aptitudes for achieving success in any field you care to mention.

What Tools Do I Need?

Okay, so you know what you want, and you think you're qualified, but you're not through yet. Do you have the necessary tools to realize your goal?

For instance, you're a New York attorney who is planning to relocate to Los Angeles. It involves a big career move, but it also means you will have to pass a California bar exam before you can practice there. If you're out of touch with current developments, you may have to spend a few months boning up for the examination.

Or, you want to sell real estate but you're not affiliated with a licensed broker; drive a truck but you don't have a truck driver's license; buy and sell securities without having passed the Securities and Exchange Commission's Registered Representative examination.

Tools can be anything from actual tools, such as those a mechanic uses to repair a car, to a license or affiliation or meeting specific requirements.

What Obstacles Do I Have to Overcome?

What about obstacles in your path? You may have everything going for you, but obstacles you didn't consider may prevent you from attaining your goal.

Obstacles fall into two broad categories, personal and practical. In the personal sector, personality deficits can block you from realizing your goal. You may have a low stress threshold, trouble making decisions, fear of confronting new people, inability to confront problems, and so on. The above personality deficits can present monumental problems if you want to pursue sales or personnel work, marketing, or public relations.

In the practical category, you may be fighting an age barrier. Despite the Age Discrimination and Employment Act, thousands of employers prefer to hire young, aggressive, upwardly mobile types in their late twenties and early thirties as opposed to seasoned professionals in their forties and fifties. Discrimination is illegal and unfair, but nevertheless it's a given and the wise job seeker takes it into consideration. Other practical obstacles are having either too much or too little experience in your trade. Often, if you have too little experience, an employer is not interested, and if you're overqualified an employer doesn't want to touch you because he fears he can't afford you, or possibly because you'll be out the door as soon as you find a job that pays a better salary.

Write down several personal and practical obstacles that may stand in your way. Once in front of you, jot down a plan or strategy to overcome each one. Advance planning pays off. Why not be prepared for all contingencies before they occur? This will make you a more effective worker.

Find Path of Least Resistance

Once you've compatibly matched goals and abilities, you're ready to outline a path of least resistance to the career goal of your choice. First, planning is called for. Finding the path of least resistance involves creating a detailed goal chart with realizable long-term, intermediate, and short-term goals. The chart used is up to you. Some people prefer creating goal circles, which involves carving up a circle into as many goal steps as it takes to realize your goal. I prefer the horizontal goal chart because it's a little bit easier to work with.

Let's set one up. List your long-term goals on the right side of the chart. Then list your near- and intermediate-term goals on the left side.

Goal Chart		
Near Term	Intermediate	Long Term
1. Apprentice Mechanic (subgoals) a. b. c. d. e.	**2.** Group Supervisor (subgoals) a. b. c. d.	**3.** Chief Mechanic/ Liaison Officer

You're not through yet. Think carefully about all the intervening steps (or subgoals) necessary to reach each goal. List each one in the appropriate place. There may be one job step before you reach your near-term goal, two before your intermediate goal, and five before you reach home plate and your long-term objective. Naturally, the amount of goal steps will vary from individual to individual. The nice part about having a goal chart is that goals no longer seem intimidating or unmanageable. There is a world of difference between thinking about all the steps that have to be reached to attain a goal and seeing them in front of you.

Maintain a flexible attitude when setting up your goal chart. Don't hesitate to amend, add, and delete steps. Your job situation may be in a state of flux. There may be a great deal of turnover, or your company may be in the throes of a major reorganization or takeover or breakup into several divisions, any of which can alter your relationship to the company.

Set Time Frames

Some people become awfully creative and go as far as setting time frames for achieving each goal. A good deal of flexibility is needed to do this.

Adding time frames serves to put your goals in sharper perspective, and it also injects a game element into the picture. Once you put a time frame on realizing a goal, you face the challenge of meeting that deadline. *Can I do it?* All of a sudden, your skills and abilities are put to the test.

However, don't be disappointed if you don't meet that goal in the specified time. If your goal is to be named district manager over a sixteen-month period and you find that it can't be done in less than two years, don't give up. Consider the situation carefully. Possibly there were other variables you failed to consider when you created your goal chart, or, more likely, your job situation changed over the past year. Whatever the reasons, revise your chart, and create new time frames. It's that simple.

Take a look at the sample chart with enclosed time frames. Including months is optional but they can be handy if promotions occur at different times of the year.

Goal Chart (October 4, 1985)		
Near Term	Intermediate	Long Term
1. Apprentice Mechanic Sept. 1985 a. Mechanic Helper Jan. 1986 b. Mechanic Assistant Sept. 1986 c. Mechanic Sept. 1987	2. Group Supervisor Jan. 1988 a. Control Supervisor Jan. 1989 b. Maintenance Supervisor Sept. 1990	3. Chief Mechanic Jan. 1991

Have a Sense of Mission

Intimately entwined with setting realistic goals is having a sense of mission. Goal and mission fit together like a hand and glove. The task to be completed, or mission, is the desired goal at the end of the tunnel. It's just another way of looking at the same coin. Having a sense of mission takes your goal out of the humdrum accomplishment-oriented world and gives it a special aura and purpose. It adds romance and adventure to your goal package.

Wrapping your goal around a mission makes the game all the more exciting. What better way to liven things up than to make you the star of your own show. Every once in a while step out of reality and let your imagination have free rein. On a mere whim, add or subtract characters, try to charge through a special goal course with demanding time frames and objectives only you can meet.

The more you think about it, the more creative you can be. The creative person comes to the conclusion that only he is responsible for his fate. If he wants things to happen, he has to make them happen. He can't be naive and think someone is going to come along and spice up the plot so he can dash through the finish line with thousands of trumpets blaring Purcell's "Trumpet Voluntary." Nice fantasy indeed, but it's not going to happen. That's analogous to crowds of people scurrying every which way in a rainstorm to stop in unison, clasp hands, and sing "Singin' in the Rain." Only Gene Kelly could get away with that one and make it seem almost believable.

Have some fun with your goals. Make each minigoal on your goal chart one of several minimissions that have to be realized before you can move onto that superhighway leading to your final goal. Why must you be like everyone else? Why must you follow the traditional path? That's been done a trillion times before. Remember, you're special.

What Next?

We've created a goal chart and mentioned a few possible variations to consider. Now let's harness our imaginations and jump into the future to the day when your long-term goal is finally realized. Alas, you've made it. Now what? Do you empty your desk drawer, run home, pack, and head for the Florida Keys, San Diego, Palm Beach, or the back hills of Vermont to enjoy that extended vacation you've been fantasizing about for years? Nice thought, but chances are you won't want any part of it. In fact, I guarantee you won't. You've worked very hard to get this far, and you're not about to quit when the game is just getting interesting.

Naturally, you feel terrific. You've accomplished a lot. But I bet you've come to the conclusion that you're not satisfied. You thought you might be, but you're not. There is more to do, more ground to cover. You've arrived at a telling plateau in which you're both delighted and confused by your victory. Prior to this, you never thought about how you'd feel when you attained a major goal. But now that you're there, you're puzzled.

It happens every day, but each time it does, the feeling of awe and confusion that comes from reaching a goal and deciding what to do next is unique to each person. However, you'll be surprised how fast you come out of it. Rare is the person who decides to call it quits. Most of us opt to continue playing the game with just as much, and probably more, enthusiasm than we demonstrated before. Think about it for a minute. If your goal is to earn a million dollars, do you think you'll retire when you've earned that exalted figure? Did Carnegie, Mellon, Rockefeller, or Getty quit when they earned their first million? You know the answer. Their goals shifted from $1 million to $5 million, from $5 million to $10 million, until they fantasized about becoming billionaires. And it's all perfectly natural and inevitable.

What will you do when you realize your goal? Chances are you'll set new goals, work up a more enticing goal chart, and begin working toward them as avidly as you did when you contemplated your first goal chart. This time, however, you'll probably play the game as you've never played it before, with more energy, knowledge, and cunning.

TO SUM UP

1. Before creating a goal chart, carefully match your goals and abilities so they are compatible.
2. When setting up your goal chart, think in terms of a path of least resistance to each career goal.
3. Set near, intermediate, and long-term goals.
4. To make the chart as precise as possible, set subgoals (or minigoals) between each major goal target. This gives you more control over your chart.
5. For added clarity, consider setting time frames for attaining each goal. Adding time frames serves to put your goals in sharper perspective and also injects a game element into the picture.
6. Maintain a flexible attitude. Because of changing conditions and uncontrollable variables, the goal chart may have to be amended from time to time.
7. Have some fun with your goals and make each goal a mission to be completed and attained. Wrapping your goal around a mission makes the game all the more exciting.

Develop Patience and Perseverance

Some of us have high frustration levels, short tempers, and little patience, but when it comes to creation, you're going to have to train yourself to pull in the reins so you're operating at peak efficiency and producing the very best results. As we said earlier, creation is rarely the effortlessly flowing process we'd like it to be. Sometimes everything falls neatly into place and you're amazed at how simple and uncomplicated it is. But practically speaking, it requires many steps, repetition, and sometimes tedium and constant reappraisal. What you thought might take a week may take three to six months, and what you thought might involve clear-cut procedures may involve drudgery and more frustration than you bargained for.

Thousands of pertinent examples can be found. Consider the management consultant who told me about a new account where he was faced with the challenge of reducing costs and increasing profits by better than twenty-five percent. "On the surface," he says, "it looked like the perfect company. The staff was highly trained and competent and they seemed to have the right people doing all the important work. Yet senior management was justifiably concerned because the company was no longer growing at the aggressive rate it had in the past. If things don't improve, the company will begin to lose a significant part of its market share in a couple of years."

The management consultant said he felt like Sherlock Holmes in the beginning. The problem was more than clear. But where were the clues and answers? It took this conscientious consultant close to two months to find answers. And this he accomplished by spending countless days at the company, observing and speaking to everyone from truck drivers to division heads. After two months of gathering information, pieces finally fell into place. The problem was not easily detectable because senior management appeared to be savvy and on top of things. However, on close examination the consultant discovered a "good old boys" protective network at the supervisory and middle management level, which encouraged seniority and security over production and quality. Hence, production quotas were not always met, which accounted for the company's loss of part of its market share.

Here was a challenging problem that was met by painstaking fact gathering and evaluation. The creativity involved starting with nothing (no leads) and building a case that led to key sectors of the company. Data had to be gathered and interpreted, and conclusions drawn. In the beginning, he took off down blind alleys and found, after weeks of work, that he had little choice but to start over and build the puzzle from scratch.

It took longer than anticipated but the problem was solved, resulting in the firing of a number of supervisors and lower echelon workers, and of a couple of division heads, and there was an eventual improvement in the company's product line.

Thomas Edison believed firmly that perseverance leads to quality. When he was deeply involved in working on a new invention his family hardly saw him. He and his loyal crew worked around the clock, with Edison often falling asleep on his worktable in the midst of an experiment. If his meals had not been brought to him, he would have gone entire days without eating.

Unconsciously, Edison knew what the creative process entailed. It meant work, and a trial-and-error period that often lasted months. In short, perseverance. The public saw the finished product and hailed him as the genius creator who devised mind-boggling inventions that were to change the course of history. A genius he was, yet few people were aware of the exhausting amount of experimentation and research that went into each invention.

Edison, like so many creators, was a perfectionist. Even when he was satisfied with the results, he retested his hypotheses, sought advice, and made modifications so that there was no doubt in his mind about whether he could go farther. As soon as one invention was completed and patented, he went on to the next, hungry to find answers to unsolved questions that plagued him twenty-four hours a day.

Few creative people I know are ever completely satisfied with their work. Once a project is completed, it's put aside so they can move off in new directions, with greater knowledge and understanding.

Exercise

1. In terms of your own work situation, identify three weak areas (within yourself) that need improvement.
a.
b.
c.
List three areas (within yourself) with which you're pleased.
a.
b.
c.
2. What can be done to strengthen your weak areas?
a.
b.
c.
What can be done to make your strong areas stronger?
a.
b.
c.
3. Are you satisfied with your production quota?

Yes _____
No _____
If not, what can be done to improve the situation? _____
4. To increase your productivity, set a production goal _____
and a time frame in which you're going to meet it _____.

TO SUM UP

1. We're all different. Some of us have high frustration levels, short tempers, and little patience. However, when it comes to creation, train yourself to pull in the reins so that you're operating at peak efficiency and producing the very best results.
2. Perseverance leads to quality.
3. Don't expect to be completely satisfied with your work. Once a project is completed, put it aside, and move in a new direction with greater knowledge and understanding.

Take Responsibility for Your Life and Your Success

It's very easy to relegate responsibility and blame to others. Some of us develop this trait to a fine art. In large organizations, especially, we can sink into the crevices, remain inconspicuous, little more than minuscule wheels in mammoth machines. Within the plush, insulated, shiny offices of the multinational company, we can find reasons and excuses for producing as well as for not producing. Or when the product or idea is finally finished and launched, and we're not pleased with the results, we can just as easily spin on our heels and renounce it all as inaccurate, unfinished, imperfect, and marred with faults.

Even the lone individual working in isolation can find excuses and relegate blame whenever or wherever he can find a suitable rationalization. The painter who refuses to make concessions and tailor his work to the marketplace opts to suffer because he can't have things his way. He fights an infantile, idealistic battle, not realizing he'll sink into the woodwork if he doesn't make concessions. Not that he should "prostitute" his talents. However, there are many ways to approach a problem. While he may blame an insensitive world for not appreciating his skills, he fails to view the situation objectively.

He doesn't have to stop doing what he loves. But, for the sake of earning enough money to support himself, he could concentrate on producing works that are more commercial. When they begin to sell, and his cash flow improves, he can devote more time to the projects that are meaningful to him. Beyond the self-satisfaction that comes from earning money from his art, he will also be building a reputation at the same time. Our nearsighted painter doesn't realize that acceptance of his paintings (no matter how commercial) paves the way for presenting his more radical and favored artistic statements.

It's very easy to assign blame. We can find excuses for just about anything; for not painting, writing, developing a new computer program, selling, getting a better job, and just plain trying. In fact, there are millions of people who amble along blaming others for their lot in life. You probably know some yourself. The arguments and rationalizations are soon reduced to variations on all-too-common themes. "You can't get ahead, the government takes everything." "What with inflation, it's impossible to make a decent living." "You can't beat the system." "What's the point of working hard? Chances are I'll be out of a job in a year or two the way the economy is going." "Why get my hopes up? There are too many people who are better than me." "It's probably been done before, so why bother trying?" "Why study? I'm only going to fail the test anyway." On and on. Maybe you see yourself in the above. If you do, it's time to start doing something about it.

There are some lucky ones among us who start off with a definite advantage. For instance, some people are born rich and if they don't squander their money away, they'll glide through life never having to worry about supporting themselves. However, they account for only a tiny minority. And don't think for a moment that the privileged elite are without problems. But whether you're poor, middle class, or upper class, *you and only you* have final control over your existence.

There are also a number of givens that we have to contend with, many of which we have little control over. If you opt to live in a large city like New York, Chicago, or Boston, there is little you can do to buck the high rentals and escalating cost of living.

Blaming inflation and the government for your predicament is sheer nonsense. Inflation presents problems for everyone, but the majority of people not only cope with it, they manage to adjust their life styles to it. The government? Remember there are major changes every four years. This is a democracy, is it not? If you're so bothered by government policy, why don't you do something about it? Why don't you join a lobbyist group or a consumer-action committee? As for not channeling all your creative energy into your job, that's a combination of fear and lack of initiative and drive all rolled into one. Whether you work for yourself or for someone else, you're going to have to take some chances. Certainly the individual who owns his own company or who works for himself has more control over his existence than the individual who works for a large company. Nevertheless, once the corporate person adjusts to his multitiered environment, he can move in any number of directions. He can rise up the ladder, or just as easily slide to the bottommost rung and out the same door he came in. How do junior executives become senior executives and eventually chief operating officers? The answer is that they take charge of their lives, assume full responsibility for their actions, and their success, and steer themselves in any direction they choose.

What about yourself? Are you assuming full responsibility for your life so you're operating at maximum efficiency, fully utilizing your creative potential? And do you see yourself (not others) as the ultimate vehicle for achieving success in your field? If not, what can you do to change the situation?

TO SUM UP

1. Whether you work for yourself or you're part of a large organization, be careful not to blame others for your fate, or for your lot in life.
2. It's very easy to assign blame. We can find excuses and rationalizations for just about anything. See it as a cop-out for not putting your best foot forward.
3. At different points in your life, you're going to have to step outside yourself and take chances.
4. Only you can assume full responsibility for your success and steer yourself in the direction you choose.

Believe in Yourself

There are two states of mind that accompany the early stages of creativity. One state of mind approaches a problem with the attitude, *I'm going to do this no matter what, and I don't care how long it takes.* The other state of mind feels, *Oh well, I'll give it a shot. I don't know whether it will work or not, but I guess I have nothing to lose.*

Which one is more apt to result in realization of a goal? If you said the first, you're on target. Knowing that there are going to be obstacles along the way, and that it may take a long time to realize your goals, you're determined to do whatever has to be done to cross the finish line.

The latter frame of mind is not sure of itself. Before a project begins, it's already cushioning itself for failure. One is positive, assertive, and sure of itself, the other is insecure and doubtful. The first one is success bound, the second is failure bound.

The two attitudes can be likened to having the option of boarding one of two trains scheduled to leave for the same destination. One train is new, sleek, and fast, the other is older, slower, and in need of repair. The fare on the faster train, however, is slightly more than the fare on the slower one.

Of course, you can save money by taking the slower, cheaper train. But look what you're getting and risking by making that decision. The train is old, and it is more likely to break down than the newer one. A breakdown means you'll be arriving at your destination hours late, which could mean a loss of precious work time. And if you're paid on an hourly basis, you could lose a great deal of money if the train breaks down frequently. The old train is also not as comfortable as the newer one.

Now consider the advantages of taking the faster train. It's in excellent condition and you're almost guaranteed to get to your destination on time, and maybe even ahead of schedule. Since it's comfortable and a pleasant place to be, you may be inspired to work while traveling. Finally, there is the pleasure and comfort of traveling in an anxiety-free state. This contrasts with riding the old train and wondering, *Will I get there on time? I can't risk walking into work two hours late again!*

When you consider the advantages of taking the faster train, the slight difference in fares no longer seems significant. Most important is the state of mind that guides you in making your decision. Again, we come back to familiar phrases, negative versus positive, success versus failure. If you're success oriented and maintain a positive frame of mind, in seconds you'll size up a situation like the one described above. Simple reasoning guides you in coming to a pragmatic conclusion. Instead of circling the periphery, you immediately go to the heart of the issue, rather than focusing on small, insignificant issues.

The action-oriented person weighs the facts and decides immediately that the fast train is the best bet. Coming to the problem with a success-motivated frame of mind, the important whys behind the decision are more than apparent.

It all simmers down to a couple of important questions. What kind of decisions are you going to make, and how and where are you going to invest your energy? The clear-thinking individual sees things in logical perspective. He doesn't let doubt and negative feelings get in his way. He starts out wholeheartedly believing in his abilities and powers. His energy is targeted and directed, like an arrow about to pierce the center of a target. It's not "I think I will get it done," but "I will get it done." Say these two sentences out loud and you'll see that there is a world of difference between them. One is passive, the other is action oriented.

Right alongside the action-oriented frame of mind is the belief that anything is possible once you dedicate yourself to the task. Compared to wish, belief is a much stronger word. Believing something can be done will propel you forward, creating the momentum to complete the task. A belief in the impossible will guide you along fascinating never-before-traveled highways. Along the way your ideas may be altered to reflect new insights and in the end, your results may not correspond to your original premise. This is to be expected. When this happens, don't lose sight of your mission to break new ground. A strong belief will lead you to the strategy necessary to solve the problem at hand.

And even if you don't believe you can accomplish something, act as though you do. Soon enough, you'll see results and a change in attitude will follow. Your actions and accomplishments will be proof enough that you can accomplish what you set out to do.

Believing in yourself is not the same as wishing. A wish is rooted in unrealistic fantasy. Think of all the wishes you've made or heard over the years. "I wish I had a million dollars." "I wish I could go to the moon." "I wish I had a Lamborghini." "I wish I could stop smoking." "I wish I could drop 25 pounds."

Wishing is unrealistic, purposeless thinking. There is nothing behind a wish, other than free-floating, anchorless thought, whereas strength, commitment, direction, and the knowledge to move mountains are the sturdy support beams behind belief. Belief is a power word, contrasted to wish, which is negative and shallow. Belief has a steel foundation as its base, a wish is as unsubstantial as cotton candy.

Again, look at every noteworthy invention, work of art, and scientific discovery made over the last century. There were obstacles to be hurdled, but each creator went into the ring prepared and determined to win. At the very outset, they were armed with the belief that they would succeed. And almost always that belief led to something positive, and sometimes to something unique in the form of an important discovery that affects us all.

Along with a strong belief in your abilities, a positive attitude is an absolute must.

An awful lot has been written and said about the positive attitude. There is no point in expending more words on the subject other than to focus on how important it is in the creative process. First, a positive attitude is, by definition, a creative attitude. It is not Panglossian, but one hundred percent pragmatic. Within our vast career plan, a positive attitude keeps us within sight of our goals. Rare is the person who remains on track and moves from goal step to goal step without contending with obstacles and detours he didn't count on. They're to be expected and when they arise, alternate plans have to be made so we don't lose momentum.

It's very easy to lose touch with ourselves and be thrown unexpectedly out of sync. Just when we thought we'd be miles ahead, we find that we have to backtrack ten miles in order to chalk up a two-mile gain.

When this happens, you're not to lose sight of your creative goals. This is when a positive attitude comes to the rescue. The long and the short of it is that the only way we're going to cross the finish line is by thoroughly believing in ourselves. Giving lip service to it is not enough. You must believe in that attitude twenty-four hours a day. Once your attitude changes, the quality of your work will also change. If your attitude improves, the quality of your work will simultaneously improve as well. They work in conjunction with each other.

As Walter M. Germain puts it in *The Magic Power of Your*

Mind: "You have within you the power to do anything you desire. You have the power to change your life so that you can accomplish all the things you want of it. . . . You are the owner of a power that, when you begin to use it, will open up the road to happiness and health, to wealth and long life."

TO SUM UP

1. Don't let doubt and negative feelings get in your way.
2. Know the difference between belief and wish. Belief is a power word, wish is shallow and negative.
3. Even if you don't actually believe you can accomplish something, act as though you do. Soon enough, you'll see results, and a change in attitude will follow.
4. Never stop believing in your abilities, power, and creative potential.
5. Along with a strong belief in your abilities, a positive attitude is essential. A positive attitude is, by definition, a creative attitude.

Set Your Sights on Perfection

Regardless of your work environment, set your sights on perfection. Why *perfection*? Because it represents a clear, unobstructed end. Nothing resides beyond perfection. Don't be embarrassed to admit that perfection is an intimidating word. When you think of perfection, your mind races to the very end of the line and into the winner's circle. In the art world, Rodin's *The Thinker* has been dubbed perfect and so has Michelangelo's *David* and of course the *Mona Lisa*, along with thousands of other works of art. In the science and medical worlds, discoveries that changed the course of history and improved people's lives were also deemed perfect.

But whether any of these achievements were technically perfect will never be determined, because perfection in its final abstract sense is elusive, intangible. The perfect anything is flawless, without defect, irreproachable, and whether perfection has ever been achieved, or will ever be achieved, is a subject only philosophers and aestheticians are equipped to discuss.

For our discussion, perfection is both an objective and a subjective goal. Certainly, there are objective criteria governing, guiding, and setting standards for anything you mention, yet the objective criteria for any given work are constantly being revised in the light of new knowledge. On a subjective level, our feelings, background, and personal predispositions come into play. Given a creative work, idea, or thought, debate over whether it meets "perfect" criteria will continue as long as human beings occupy this planet.

If perfection describes the flawless, errorless, defectless product, how do we know when we've arrived at this heightened state? Even with a checklist of criteria, isn't there room for error and disagreement, no matter how slight? For every thousand individuals who stamp something perfect, I daresay there are a thousand contradicting individuals who will render the same work flawed.

Whether we ever come up with an all-encompassing definition for the word is not important. What is important is that you work *toward* perfection. Just as we mentioned the importance of setting realistic, logical goals earlier in the book, the overall goal for your creative product, whatever it is, must be perfection.

If you're content with mediocrity, your output will never amount to very much, and you'll be lucky if you distinguish yourself within your field. But if perfection is what you strive for, you're not about to settle for anything else. Eventually, you'll make your mark and work toward realizing your creative potential.

TO SUM UP

1. Set your sights on perfection.

2. The overall goal for your creative product, whatever it is, must be perfection. The elusive goal of perfection can be applied to anything you do.

3. Do not forget that perfection is both an objective and a subjective goal. For instance, there are objective criteria governing, guiding, and setting standards for anything you mention, yet the objective criteria for any given work are constantly being revised in the light of new knowledge. On a subjective level, feelings, background, and personal predispositions come into play.

Keep an Open Mind

A closed mind rejects, edits, and throws out more thoughts than it keeps; an open mind lets nothing pass it by. The creative person keeps his channels open and maintains an open mind at all times. Otherwise, his creative machinery stalls and eventually breaks down.

What about yourself? When you approach a new situation, do you prejudge it without knowing anything about it? Or do you approach it with an open mind ready to accept, learn, and study?

We all bring prejudices, beliefs, and attitudes to a situation. But it is the aware person who is in touch with his feelings and knows how to assess them. We're all products of our backgrounds, and our opinions are molded to a certain extent by the people around us. It's not easy but we have to learn to sort out raw data in our minds, and decide what to do with it despite our preconceptions. It's almost like sorting freshly washed laundry. Confronted with a pile of laundry, the job at hand is to separate articles of clothing, find matching pairs of socks, and fold and stack it all neatly. A similar process takes place in our minds. We sort ideas, rummage through them, and make decisions along the way. Which ones are worth holding onto; which ones are shallow and superficial; which ones need further development? Unconsciously, the process takes place all day long without abatement. Even when sleeping, the night shift in your mind is silently weighing, disseminating, and making decisions about thoughts gathered during the day.

Try to get in touch with this process, making sure the floodgates in your mind are open at all times. Don't prejudge anything until you have all the information. Before ideas can be evaluated, the mind has to gather as much information as it can and then appraise it all. Don't let subjective feelings get in your way. See them for what they are.

Look upon each day as a new learning experience. Even those of us involved in routinized jobs and life styles have the opportunity to gather new thoughts each day. The archenemy of the creative mind is stagnation. A stagnating mind atrophies and suffers from intellectual starvation. Thoughts are the mind's food. Deprive it of sustenance and it ceases to function productively. When this happens, the creative process is thwarted.

Monitor your thought processes. Welcome each day as an opportunity to gather more thoughts and learn new things. Don't let your routines stand in your way. As we said earlier, a routine or schedule is nothing more than a framework for your day. No matter how restrictive your routines, don't let yourself be imprisoned by them. Allow your mind to roam, absorb, and leap in any one of a million directions.

Remember, only you can unleash and harness your mind to optimal advantage. For creativity to take place, the mind must be free. You can imprison the body and restrict its movements, but the mind is free to travel the universe if it cares to.

TO SUM UP

1. Keep all your channels open and maintain an open mind.
2. Stay in touch with your feelings and know how to assess them.
3. Don't let subjective feelings get in your way. See them for what they are.
4. The archenemy of the creative mind is stagnation.
5. For creativity to take place the mind must be free.

Establish a Creative Atmosphere

Defining the creative atmosphere is as difficult as defining the creative worker. What is it, and where can it be found? For starters, we know that the right atmosphere is vital and that each individual requires a different set of stimuli.

Ergonomic specialists, for example, have been toying with these problems for years. Assuming the givens of a technological marketplace, they face the challenge of finding the divine harmony where man and machine work comfortably together. For the modern worker to achieve job fulfillment, ideally he should be both productive and creative—not easy accomplishments when you have workers hunched over computer terminals for hours on end performing mundane tasks.

Architects hired by major corporations have their work cut out for them. Studying all the crucial elements of a worker's surroundings, they try to find answers to the following questions: Should there be soundproof cubicles; enclosed offices with glass or wood panels; walls painted bright or conservative colors; floors, carpeted or uncarpeted; easy-listening music in the background? How close should workers be to each other? Should there be a feeling of isolation or of community?

Creating the ideal working environment is a subject that concerns every growth-minded individual and corporation. But no matter how close architects and ergonomic specialists come to designing that perfect atmosphere, it remains as elusive as achieving perfection in your work. The reasons can be traced to differences in human nature. What may be the ideal working atmosphere for one worker may be an airless prison for another.

Two New York advertising agencies, for instance, provide their copywriters with what they consider ideal working conditions. At one firm each writer has a comfortably furnished office complete with window and view, and the other has its ten copywriters spaced at comfortable intervals in a large, well-lit, carpeted room.

After spending a couple of days at each company speaking to copywriters and management, I learned that each worker was content with his setting. At the agency where copywriters had private offices, the copy chief explained it this way: "A good copywriter is worth his or her weight in gold. Without clever, imaginative, creative copy, we would close up shop. To produce good copy, you need a stimulating working environment, one that encourages and inspires you to work. For these reasons, I think it's important that our writers have comfortable, cheery offices with good desks and typewriters, and a window and view, when possible. Our people must agree because the quality of work has been consistently high and turnover low."

On the other hand, the copy chief at the agency with the city room–type atmosphere expresses another view. "Since creativity is not something you can turn off and on at will, we've discovered that it's important to create an atmosphere that almost forces one writer to work with or assist another. Since many of our detailed programs require a collaborative effort, having our copywriters in one room encourages both group and individual creativity. Writers have the best of both worlds. If a writer wants to work undisturbed by himself he can, or if he needs the assistance of another, he merely pivots his swivel chair and asks for it. I've also discovered that this type of atmosphere is not only more realistic, it's also healthier. Since all the workers are close to each other, they can seek advice without embarrassment. When writers are closeted in offices, they often feel compelled to go it alone and not rely too heavily on fellow writers. In ad writing, that kind of disciplined stoicism often leads to writer's block and an inconsistent output. However, the stronger the group effort, the better the results."

This copy chief also added that his writers seem content and that turnover at his firm was slight. Now the inevitable question: Which is the more creative atmosphere? Answer: Depending upon your personality, both can be equally creative.

Think of the above examples in terms of yourself. If you were a copywriter, which firm would you choose? Maybe you consider one setting stifling and claustrophobic and the other charged, exciting, and free.

One more example. Two writers I know work in totally different settings. Both live in the New York suburbs and each one has his own way of working. We'll call one Ed and the other John. Ed kisses his wife goodbye and heads for his attic office to work undisturbed for eight hours. The office has a rustic simplicity—cozy, small, efficient. Everything Ed needs is within reach. A large oak desk sits at a strategic angle facing the room's one window, which looks out on a quiet street. On the desk is a telephone, a typewriter, and neatly stacked piles of paper. Filing cabinets are symmetrically placed on either side of the desk. To give the room a living room/den—type atmosphere, at the far end of the room is a small sofa with pillows and a reading light.

While Ed is getting ready to work, John is making his way to his rented one-room office in Manhattan. He has a congenial arrangement with an attorney and an accountant where he rents the small office for a modest monthly rental. Where every piece of furniture in Ed's office was meticulously chosen, everything in John's office is rented, except the sleek new Olivetti electric typewriter that he bought a year ago. The large metal desk looks like it has seen better days, and the same goes for the filing cabinets and office chairs.

Let's look at these work settings a little bit closer. Ed and John are writers who work in seclusion. Yet their surroundings are very different. Ed explains, "I can't work just anywhere. I need seclusion, but it has to be a special kind of seclusion. This is why I converted the attic into an office. It takes me a long time to get started and the only way I can rev myself up is to be by myself for long periods of time. That's why I do everything in my power to get my creative motor going as quickly as possible. Every day I'm in my office at eight-fifteen to eight-thirty. If I'm lucky, I start getting down to serious work by ten or ten-thirty. Other times I don't start cooking until eleven or eleven-thirty. If I'm disturbed, or I'm distracted by noise or people, I lose hours."

To get work done, Ed says discipline is essential. "Most days I remain in my office for six or seven hours at a time. I take a large thermos of coffee, a couple of sandwiches, so I'm not sidetracked during the day."

John has a different philosophy about working. "I tried working in my home, but it didn't work. It's not that it wasn't quiet or there were too many distractions. The problem was it was too quiet. After four or five hours, it started to get me down. I needed a change in scenery, I need to see and hear people. That's why I took the office in the city. It worked out well because it is exactly what I need. It provides just the right change in scenery, enabling me to put in a productive day's work. Even though I spend two hours commuting, I've discovered that I'm more productive working this way than I was when I worked in my home. I look forward to the trip to and from work on the railroad. It breaks up the day nicely. I read the newspaper, and get my thoughts in order. When I get to my office I'm charged and ready to begin work. During the day I usually leave the office at around one or two in the afternoon to get a sandwich or a slice of pizza. Even if it's just a fifteen-minute break, I find that I need a change of scenery."

As far as interacting with people, John says he needs people in his "creative periphery." "I often go an entire week without speaking to others during the day," he says. "I do my best work when I'm alone. But I like to know there are people around me. On occasions I enjoy taking a midday break and walking in crowds and bumping into people in elevators. That kind of superficial contact is very relaxing."

John added that his office accouterments are not that important to him. It matters little whether his desk is old or new, wood or metal. "As long as I can work on it," he laughs. The only thing he insists upon is a good typewriter.

The examples illustrate that each of us needs a different kind of atmosphere in order to be creative. However, the majority of workers have little control over their atmosphere. Our work environment is given to us ready-made and it's up to us either to accept it and make the best of it, try and modify it, or if all else fails, try to change it.

I'm not suggesting that everyone not working under optimally creative conditions quit their jobs. Not only is it unrealistic, it's also not feasible, especially in this tough job market. What you *can* do, however, is take a hard look at your work atmosphere to determine whether it encourages or discourages creativity.

Answer the following questions:

1. What is it about your atmosphere that you like? Dislike?
2. Does it encourage creativity?
3. Do you have any control over it?
4. Can you relate your work atmosphere to your creativity quotient?
5. What conditions do you need to work to your creative potential?
6. What constructive changes can you make in your environment to augment your creativity?

Unless we work on an assembly line, most of us can alter our work environment slightly, enough to make a difference. We can't demand plush carpeted offices and Vivaldi droning in the background, but we can make subtle changes that can improve our attitude and thus make us more productive and creative in our work. Within limitations, we can build an atmosphere that is maximally creative.

You'd be surprised what little alterations in our work setting can do. Consider the following:

1. *Change the lighting.* Is your desk lamp adequate? A brighter light can make a world of difference. Not only will you see a lot better, but a great deal of light can turn a depressing atmosphere into a cheery one.

2. *What about the position of your desk?* For variety's sake, change its position, or its angle.

3. *Is your desk a cluttered mess?* This can make it almost impossible to get things done. Invest an hour or more of your time and clean it up. It may inspire you to put more effort into your work and be more productive. As a result, your creativity is bound to improve as well. Instead of being greeted by a messy, cluttered desk in the morning, you'll find order instead. You may be surprised to discover that your day begins on a positive note. You

can begin work immediately instead of spending twenty minutes trying to get your act together.

4. *Are you faced with bare, nondescript walls?* Without creating a major commotion, couldn't you hang a poster or a painting to liven up your work station? Would anyone mind?

The above are only suggestions. Possibly, there are other things you can do to make your work environment more inspiring. Awareness is half the battle. Once in touch with the fact that something is off and change is needed, you can set the wheels in motion and rectify the situation.

TO SUM UP

1. Our work environment is given to us ready-made. We can either accept it or try to modify it.

2. Most of us don't realize we have the power to alter our work environment to a certain extent.

3. We can, for example, make moderate alterations— change the lighting and position of our desks, and so on.

4. Awareness is half the battle. Don't let a discouraging work environment hamper your output or creativity. Within reason, do what you can to overcome it.

Now that we've laid the groundwork for creativity, let's explore 20 ways to be more creative in our work.

PART II

20 WAYS TO BE MORE CREATIVE IN YOUR JOB

CHAPTER 1
FIND YOUR
TARGET

Discovering your creativity is a first step. You're in touch with your creativity, now what? How do you market it, profit from it? How do you actually become more creative in your job?

Think of yourself as a potential asset to any growth-minded company or organization and figure out where your creativity will have maximum impact.

Targeting your creativity is the kickoff point in the creative process. It's the beginning, pointing up the necessity for starting off on the right foot. Think of yourself as a pro football player who has just been handed the ball. The opposing team is charging right for you. Where is the path of least resistance? Where lies the mystical track that leads to your goal and victory?

Fine-tune your creative direction and target yourself toward your goals. You face options, choices, decisions; which path do you take, what do you want to accomplish?

Whatever you do, don't go off half-cocked. Get the lay of the land before deciding on a course of action. Think of yourself as the general of a mighty army surveying the battlefield considering a variety of battle plans. Which one will be most effective? Which is the safest, fastest, and easiest to expedite?

Finding that special place where you're going to unleash your creativity is not a life-and-death situation, but why waste time if you don't have to. Pause, reflect, and consider the options before you figure out where creativity is needed and will be welcomed.

The creative person has a lot more freedom than he is aware of. Unlike a lot of other people, he doesn't see himself locked into situations with no escape routes available. Instead, many creative paths lie before him. The trick is setting out on the right one.

Let's do a fast inventory. We know what our overall goal is, and we've laid the groundwork for creativity. We're fueled and ready to go. Now we have to begin the exciting relay race by finding out where in our company or field of endeavor our creativity is most needed.

Answer the following questions:

1. Where is there a problem left unsolved? A system that doesn't work? A better way of doing things?
2. To which project should I apply my creative abilities?
3. What idea, or problem, is most viable? Which one stands the best chance of being realized? Which one deserves my immediate attention?
4. Where will my talents and abilities be most valued?

Once you have answers to the above questions, you know what has to be done. Finding out where the problems lie automatically puts you at the beginning of the creative process. You've found the problem to be solved—the seed from which creativity will grow. You're ready to begin.

CHAPTER 2
GET
ORGANIZED

What are the first things you notice when you walk into the kitchen of a gourmet chef and the laboratory of a research scientist? You don't see the connection? Think about it for a second or two because the connection is more than clear.

Time is up. The answers are order and cleanliness. These are essential for cook and scientist to be creative and turn out their best work.

In order for the scientist to achieve the desired results, he must have the right working conditions. The right conditions include a fully equipped laboratory, and a method of doing research and conducting experiments that produces accurate work. The scientist carefully prepares his experiments, tests his data, and evaluates his results. In other words, throughout the scientific process, order is paramount if reliable creative work is to take place.

Now let's drop in on our gourmet chef. Ah yes, who can resist those delicious, mouth-watering smells wafting through the air. One thing is for sure, you're not going to find them in the research scientist's laboratory. But there are many similarities. The chef's kitchen is just as neat and orderly as the scientist's laboratory. In fact, the kitchen is so immaculate that you could eat off the floor. Next, note how the kitchen is set up. I daresay it's not like your kitchen when you are trying to concoct one of those savory recipes in the *New York Times Cookbook*, where every spice, herb, pot, and pan is sprawled over every inch of counter space in your kitchen. Aside from the fact that clutter and mess are aesthetically unpleasing, chefs simply can't afford to be slovenly. If they expect to be creative and feed the hundreds of people clamoring for their sirloin steaks, trout amandine, bouillabaisse, stuffed shrimps, veal marsala, and curries, they have to run a tight ship.

Most chefs are fanatical about order. Everything is in the right place and if something is used, be it a spice, vegetable, or portion of meat, the unused portion is promptly returned to its proper place.

Whether you're a cook, scientist, salesperson, clerk, secretary, financial planner, or politician, order is essential if you hope to do your job well and generate maximum creativity in the process.

Before we outline steps to help you create order, let's evaluate your work habits and work environment.

1. Do you flounder for twenty minutes deciding what has to be done? Do you initially feel like you're all over the place, scattered and without grounding?

2. Do you experience an initial feeling of anxiety because you don't know what to tackle first?

3. Do you try to do ten things at once, in an effort to get everything done quickly?

If your answer is yes to all of the above, please don't make a mad dash for the nearest window. Believe me, you're not alone. You're one of millions. In this fast-paced world of ours many of us feel like we're on treadmills, out of control and compelled to get things done more quickly than it's possible. When you feel this way, pause for a few seconds, put the world back in place, and realize that you'll accomplish little going off in a million directions at once. All you'll succeed in doing is making yourself nervous, tense, and irritable. Calm down and proceed logically, carefully, and with a system.

Let's find the divine harmony that will make our lives so much easier, happier, and more creative. It takes a while to put together a harmonious work environment, and each of us faces different problems and obstacles. Nevertheless, the following general questions will help you improve your work environment and increase your efficiency and creativity considerably.

1. *What equipment, or accessories, do you need?* Whether you're an auto mechanic or a secretary, you need the accessories of your trade before you begin work. The mechanic needs a precision set of tools, lubricating oils, grease, rags, work clothes, and a number of other accessories. The secretary needs a typewriter (or word processor), telephone, correction fluid, pens, pencils, erasers, stationery, copy paper, carbon paper, paper clips, stapler, and a dozen or more other accessories. You'd be surprised at all the nitty-gritty ingredients we all need to get our work done.

A reporter who runs out to cover a story without a pen and notebook is out of luck. Not only will she not get her story, she'll probably lose her job in the bargain.

2. *Is your equipment readily available?* Can you get to it quickly? Think about all the time you waste searching for pencils, pens, paper clips, or a telephone number you thought you placed on the right side of your desk, or under your blotter.

3. *Do you have a flexible order or system to process the work at hand?* Unconsciously, we perform our work in some kind of order. Get in touch with that order, analyze it, and understand it. Can it be tightened or improved so that you're more efficient, productive, and creative?

Now you're moving. You've implemented your systems, you're accomplishing more, and you have more opportunities to use your creativity. Terrific. I know you feel a lot better. You're not through, though. There is one more thing to do. To avoid what can often be a lengthy startup time in the morning, take the following precautions at the end of your day, before closing up shop and charging for the door.

1. *Create an informal work plan for the next day.* You probably can't do it for the entire day, but I bet you can do it for the first

couple of hours. When we start work in the morning, most of us pick up where we left off. However, many workers spend up to forty-five minutes getting their bearings deciding what has to be done first. On a piece of paper, establish a five-step plan of things that have to be done and a suggested order for doing them.

2. *Think about your priorities for the next day.* One of the priorities may be on your five-step plan. If it is, star it so you know it's important and demands special attention. If it's not part of the five-step plan, place a bullet or asterisk under the list and jot down your priority items. This way, when you crawl into work the next morning, groggy and wondering what to tackle first, all you have to do is scan your list and you'll be productive within ten or fifteen minutes. The list is worth the effort, and it's a habit that should be developed. It dramatically decreases your start-up time and, by the end of the week, your productivity and your creativity will increase noticeably.

CHAPTER 3
DISCIPLINE
YOURSELF

For our purposes, there are two types of discipline, inner and outer discipline. Let's start with *outer* discipline, which is a lot easier to come to terms with.

Many of the disciplines of the outside world come to us ready-made. There is little we can do about them. We can gripe, get angry, and rebel, but sooner or later we have to come around and obey the rules.

As children, we're exposed to discipline early. Try our parents' patience up to a point and they explode. Toss the hot oatmeal in mom's face and you can count on a firm slap on the hand, and then back into the crib to cool off for an hour or so.

The disciplinary process continues throughout our lives. You can't have an effective educational system without clear-cut disciplinary measures. Cut classes, cheat on exams, and you can expect to be called on the carpet. The disciplinary measures range from a mild talking-to or vehement reprimand to suspension from school.

That's one kind of outer discipline. Society at large has its disciplines as well. There are laws designed to protect us. Violate one of them and you risk disciplinary action. Cheat someone and you face a heavy fine, humiliation, and possibly a small jail sentence. Disregard a driving regulation and you risk losing your license. Shoot someone and you can wind up with a life's prison sentence, or face losing your life in the electric chair or gas chamber.

And there are the outer disciplines imposed by your job. Whether you work for a small two-person business, a small corporation employing one hundred people, or an international conglomerate, you can't escape rules—lots of them. Disobey those rules and you'll face disciplinary action, depending upon the severity of your indiscretion. If you're late too often, you risk losing a small percentage of your pay; take too many sick days in a given year and your vacation will be curtailed by a couple of days; don't show up for work for an extended period of time and you'll lose your job; skim money from your expense account to renovate your home and risk being barred from working in your industry.

These are just a few of the outward disciplines we have to cope with. Yet, if you're talking about creativity, you have to go beyond the outward disciplines and focus on *inner* discipline, which is a lot different. For creativity to take place, inner discipline is essential. Inner discipline implies focusing all your energy on the creative task. It means not wandering off into space at the mere thought of doing the job at hand or finding something else to do or breaking up the task into a thousand bite-size units so it is palatable and extended over a long period of time.

The question is, How do you become disciplined? From speaking to people in different vocations, I learned that many creative people employ disciplinary rituals just prior to getting down to the serious work at hand.

A systems analyst we spoke to starts thinking about a project an hour before he actually gets down to work. The thinking process usually begins just after he gets back from lunch. Once his mind focuses, he sits down to work at about three and continues to hack away at difficult analytical problems until he's made headway. Sometimes he walks away from his desk at five-thirty, other times he loses track of time and doesn't quit until eight.

A daily newspaper columnist closes his office door, shuts the blinds to block out the sunlight, lights the first of a long stream of cigarettes, and begins to peck away at tomorrow's column. It's a daily ritual.

A supervising switching technician at American Telephone & Telegraph goes through the same routine every day. Before he goes about the time-consuming task of problem solving and trouble-shooting, he systematically clears his desk. Each paper and object is carefully removed and placed on an adjoining table so he can have enough room to study blueprints and computer printouts. The process takes about half an hour and during that period his mind darts about and prepares to tackle the problems at hand. When he is finally ready to begin, his mind is activated, his attention is focused, and he's raring to go.

A top dress designer religiously closets herself in her office between ten and eleven every morning. A container of coffee is sent to her, the door is closed, and she sips her coffee and paces up and down her office in order to get the creative juices flowing.

Many more examples can be cited. Each one involves an inner disciplinary ritual that encourages thoughts and ideas to bubble to the surface. The discipline is self-imposed, as opposed to outer directed. Each of the individuals cited created his or her own disciplinary routine in order to accomplish something positive. Each routine wasn't imposed whenever the right mood struck. Instead, it was incorporated within daily work routines.

An easy way to understand the difference between outer and inner discipline is to view them as a circle within a circle. The outward circle represents the disciplines of your work environment (or outside world) and the inner circle is the discipline you impose on yourself in order to channel your creativity.

A self-employed individual, on the other hand, doesn't face the problem of adjusting his creative rhythms to an organization. He can arrange his day any way he sees fit. Nevertheless, he faces a bigger challenge in having to carve up large blocks of time so he can discipline his creative energies and be effective in his work.

From whatever angle you approach the subject of creativity, discipline is essential for the creative product to be born.

Here are some tips to help you become more disciplined:

1. *Find a compatible disciplinary exercise or ritual to focus your attention.* Find something you enjoy doing that can be done simply and quickly. Obviously, you can't expect to play basketball or hockey or jog just prior to starting work.

2. *Don't be lazy and procrastinate.* Employ the above exercise routinely. Soon enough, it will become habit.

3. *Come to terms with your outer and inner disciplines.* A good way to get in touch with them is to isolate some of the outer and inner disciplines that make up your life, as shown in the example below.

Outer Discipline	Inner Discipline
1. Reporting to work at nine a.m.	1. Working toward realistic career goals
2. Paying city, state, and federal taxes on time	2. Building support systems
3. Obeying the law	3. Realizing your creativity

Take a look at the example below. A fictitious mechanical engineer took a hard look at the inner and outer disciplines of his life and came up with the following chart.

Outer Disciplines
1. Obeying the law
2. Paying taxes
3. Cooperating with neighbors
4. Getting membership in school/church groups, and so on
5. Voting regularly
6. Participating in local government groups
7. Reporting to work at nine a.m.

Inner Disciplines

1. Being the best at job
2. Forming support groups
3. Keeping up with industry developments
4. Constantly working to improve self
5. Realizing higher production quota
6. Working toward realizing successive career goals
7. Designing new process for increasing machine tool production
8. Convincing top brass that above process can be marketed on global scale

Try the above exercise. You may find that your list contains fifteen or twenty different disciplines in each category. However many steps, it's a good way to look at your obligations closely.

CHAPTER 4
UNLEASH
YOUR
IMAGINATION

"Imagination is more important than knowledge," said Albert Einstein. And, according to Montaigne, "A strong imagination begetteth opportunity."

Creativity and imagination go hand in hand. Without imagination, the creative person would not be able to visualize, fantasize about, and harness ideas. Imagination is the heart, soul, and nucleus of the creative process. Without it, creativity could not take place.

Think about your creativity and the creativity of those around you. What do you see? A common thread can be found. It matters little what type of creativity we're talking about. Whether it's an idea, mathematical formula, work of art, or scientific theory, someone's imagination triggered the creative process.

While *imagination* has been defined a hundred different ways, the simplest definition is that it leads to a confrontation with the problem at hand. And it matters little what the problem is. Simply, imagination is the ability to spot gaps and inadequacies that others fail to see. The creative person is disturbed by those gaps, or inadequacies, and works to find ways to close them. In other words, he sees problems where others are content to maintain the status quo.

In *Art as Experience*, John Dewey defines imagination as "a way of seeing and feeling things as they compose an integral world. It is the large and generous blending of interests at the point where the mind comes in contact with the world. When old and familiar things are made new in experience, there is imagination." And in *Meaning and Truth in the Arts*, John Hospers says that "imagination is the outstanding and distinguishing characteristic of artistic creation."

That's only one part of the story. To expand Hospers' definition, it's safe to say that imagination is the distinguishing characteristic of all creation. If it were not for someone's imagination, I wouldn't be pecking away at this manuscript on a high-speed IBM typewriter. I'd be writing the book in longhand, adding months to the manuscript's preparation. And if we didn't have computerized typesetting, and sleek high-volume presses, the production of the book could take an additional six to eight months.

The history of man is the history of creativity in action. The impetus behind every creative accomplishment can be traced to someone's imagination. Take the discovery of the wheel and fire. They seem like simple accomplishments in the face of all that followed, yet they opened doors that triggered more questions, which led to still greater discoveries. The more questions to answer, the more there is to do and accomplish.

Each invention and discovery leads to something new. Each conquest serves as a tasty hors d'oeuvre for the creative imagination. It whets the appetite, making it abundantly clear that something more has to be done.

Just as we owe our progress to the imaginative powers of human beings, it is our imagination that is going to propel us toward new frontiers. If you're content to rely on the imagination of others, you'll be just another worker biding time until five o'clock and a Friday paycheck. All you'll be doing is benefiting from the accomplishments of others—the farsighted individuals who started your company, and organized the tiers of authority over you. But the moment you step back from the group and see things in a new, compelling, and thought-provoking light, you will have ignited the fires of your own imagination.

In terms of your ultimate success, it's crucial that you know you have the power to distinguish yourself. Your imagination can put you on a new plateau. What distinguishes a mediocre systems analyst from an outstanding one, an average salesperson from a super salesperson, or an ordinary accountant from an enterprising one? Answer: Imagination. The outstanding systems analyst is going to devise systems that offer something unique, whereas a mediocre systems analyst will do things the way they've always been done. The super salesperson will not stop until he finds creative approaches to entice clients to buy his products, thus making him a cut above the average. And an enterprising accountant will distinguish himself by devising systems that save his clients money by reducing their tax bite.

Think of imagination as an integral part of the creative relay race. It is imagination that starts the race with a thunderous bang. After that it's up to you to channel your creative energy in the right direction so that you can eventually dart over the finish line first, thus completing the creative process.

The best way to sharpen your imagination is to use it constantly, not just in the work setting, but every chance you get. Remember your imagination is unlike anyone else's. Your neighbor may have painted three landscapes, written five books, and renovated his entire house, but your imagination is just as rich and active as his. And who's to say it's not more unique?

All day long there are hundreds of opportunities to challenge and fire your imagination. Let's find out what they are by carving a day into four blocks of time. Time is spent:

1. At home
2. On the move
3. At work
4. At play

Within these four situations, there are two scenarios to contemplate. One is the real situation, the other is the one you imagine or create. Relax and let yourself go. This is your show and you can do anything you want. You can let your imagination go as far as it possibly can, or you can create situations, events, things, and experiences that are expanded wishes, and extensions of real life situations.

Start *at home*. Like all of us, you're faced with a succession of tedious chores and responsibilities that have to be done on a daily, or weekly, basis. Housework, for one, is an annoying chore. So, for some, is cooking. If you could have your way, you'd change things. What would you do? What else but create a push-button house run by computers, and self-sufficient robots. Before leaving for work in the morning, you would effortlessly throw a series of switches, programming the house for the entire day. At the appointed hour, the roast automatically begins to simmer in its own juices and the soufflé and home-baked bread are regulated separately. Fifteen minutes before you walk into the house martini glasses are chilled; as you walk up the front stairs the exact proportions of gin and vermouth fill the chilled glass to the right level, making the perfect extra dry martini; and at the last millisecond, an olive drops into the frosty liquid. All you have to do is drink it.

Throughout the day, your trusted robot cleans the house, does the laundry, orders groceries from the store, and, if there is any time left, repairs the leaky roof and damaged storm windows.

How's that for an active imagination? If it were only true.

Traveling to work? Your imagination comes to the rescue. What can be done about the annoying crowds? The reality is nothing very much, but your imagination can temporarily improve the situation by eliminating them from your field of vision. One minute they're there, the next you're a lone survivor enjoying the comfort and freedom of roaming your enormous city by yourself. Extraordinary thought, you ponder. *What if?* Not only do you have the subways and buses to yourself, but every vehicle on the street is yours. Not just the Chevys, Fords, and Buicks, but the Ferraris, Lamborghinis, Jaguars, and Bentleys. And what about the banks and fantastic stores? They're all yours. It's utopia, with power, freedom, and everything you've ever dreamed and wanted. It's hard to come down from a vision like that. Don't let your imagination go too far, because inevitably you'll have to come back to earth and make your way to work with crowds and the million and one annoyances you have to contend with every day. Nevertheless, your imagination can take the sting, tedium, and boredom out of everyday events. By changing your frame of mind, it can add a sense of adventure and newness to your day.

At work? Here's where your imagination can do wonders. To appreciate how extraordinary and unusual it is, it's important to start from home base and realistically appraise your situation.

Take a look at your work. What do you see? Remember, be objective. Your eyes are cameras, your ears are tapes recorders, your mind is capturing the entire scene so you can ponder it all and decide on a course of action.

When searching for a target for your creativity (mentioned in Part Two, Chapter One), your imagination comes to the rescue by helping you latch on to the most viable one, the one that stands the best chance of being realized.

Regardless of how you use your imagination, think of it as operating a two-stage lever. First, it considers the imponderable; second, the conquerable. In this two-stage process, a world of choices, suggestions, and options open up for you. You have the world at your disposal.

In other areas of our lives we don't have to be all that pragmatic. We can afford to let our imaginations create impossible situations (fantasy house and car, lone survivor image), but at work we must function in the real world and set our sights on tangible goals. That doesn't mean we shouldn't exploit our imaginations. The difference is that our imaginations should be focused toward realizable objectives.

For instance, you're a systems analyst with big dreams. You're all of 22 and you just started your first major job working as a lowly assistant for a multimillion-dollar computer manufacturer. After a tedious break-in period, where you were introduced to the staff and fully indoctrinated, your imagination begins to work overtime. Dreams and fantasies begin to collide like out-of-control meteorites; your imagination concocts extraordinary situations. One minute you're doing your lowly job the best you can, the next you're introducing new software packages; your unique ideas are revolutionizing the very fabric of the industry. It's quite a picture. Can it be realized? Is your imagination far too active and unrealistic? Are you one of millions of dreamers who will never do anything more than take solace in fantasies created by an overzealous imagination? I hope not. Let me again remind you that every great invention, theory, principle, or revolutionary tenet started with someone's rich imagination. A belief in your abilities, combined with a burning desire to make the impossible come true, and the imagined situation and reality can be bridged.

More realistically, you see gaps and holes that need to be filled. And you're the one who can fill those gaps.

The more you think about it, the quicker you realize that you have the talent and knowledge to eventually design new software packages. Yes, you can be a ground breaker, and your ideas can have a vast impact on your industry. It can all be accomplished, *if* you dedicate yourself to the task.

At play? The same principles apply. Your imagination can create any number of enticing scenarios. An amateur tennis player imagines she's a touring professional, claiming extraordinary fees, and traveling the globe like a jet-setter. Her imagination creates an impossible situation that has a positive impact on her game. She won't play as well as Tracy Austin, but the imagined scenario may perk up her game considerably.

We've touched on only a few examples. Take chances and *unleash* your imagination. Your imagination knows no boundaries. It is not trapped by rules, schedules, and conventional thinking. It can roam and explore the heavens and earth and accomplish great things.

What does all of the above have to do with using your imagination to be more creative on your job? Answer: Everything. We've created different scenarios to show the importance of constantly using your imagination, not just on the job, but everywhere, in every conceivable situation. The idea is to use your imagination constantly. Whatever you do, don't let it atrophy. It's as valuable and necessary as hands, ears, eyes, and limbs. Let it stretch, bend, be free, agile, expressive, and expansive. What most of us fail to realize is that constant use of our imaginations in myriad situations extends to all facets of our lives. Let's go back to Albert Einstein's quote, "Imagination is more important than knowledge." In the light of new information, is it not true?

CHAPTER 5
VISUALIZE
YOUR GOAL

Think of each creative idea as an embryo, or as an amorphic form that is about to assume a shape and identity all its own.

Remember, creativity always begins with an idea. However, see that idea for what it is. It's alive, but it's also fragile and, if it's not properly nurtured, it will perish.

It matters little whether your idea is good, great, or even brilliant. In the final analysis, it is only a first step, I've met countless people who had fantastic ideas for making money, or ideas for novels or movies that sounded like surefire successes. Each time an idea was proposed to me I responded by saying, "Sounds great. Why don't you have a shot at it?" Nine out of ten times, that's as far as the idea went. It's analogous to a baseball player blasting a ball into center field with no one on the field to catch it. The ball takes off like a rocket and seconds later it lands in the grass with a dull thud. So it goes with millions of great ideas.

That great idea of yours is not going to materialize by itself. You have to feed it, take care of it, love it, shape it until it is whole, strong, and sustainable. An important primary step in breathing life into an idea is visualizing it. In other words, think about it, picture it, and focus on it until it's crystal clear. By so doing, you're fueling the creative process, convincing yourself that an idea, premise, or concept can actually be taken through its various stages and developed so it sees the light of day. Think of visualization as a telescopic tool, accurately describing in great detail the dimensions and ramifications of your idea. It is a most important adjunct to the creative process. Not only does it excite and motivate you to go further, it also focuses and channels your energy, providing necessary direction to take your idea through the essential creative stages.

Webster's New Collegiate Dictionary defines visualization as "the formation of mental visual images." True enough. But let's develop the visualization process further. First, there are no all-purpose visualization routines to apply to all work situations. It's up to you to harness the visualization process in your own way and on your own terms.

Millions of us unconsciously employ visualization in problem-solving situations without realizing it. However, you stand a better chance of developing your idea if you're conscious of the multistage process.

Visualization can be likened to an emerging picture. First, it is no more than a simple outline. Progressively, it moves to a two-dimensional shape and eventually becomes three dimensional. That wavering, tottering, once fragile idea has grown and is ready to be tested.

I'm going to show you how to use visualization to increase your productivity and sharpen your creative powers. Below, we've outlined six stages in the visualization process.

1. Mobilize yourself
2. Develop your idea
3. Let it become a vague picture
4. See and feel details
5. Talk to your characters
6. Believe in your visualized idea

1. *Mobilize yourself.* You can try your hand at visualization anywhere: walking to work, sitting on a train, while waiting for a social or business appointment. For best results, however, I suggest peace and quite. Why rush the process, or, worse yet, why interrupt it when it gets exciting and you're gaining insights? If you're considering a great idea, you're doing it a disservice by charging through the visualization process. It's analogous to gulping down a vintage wine. That's an unpardonable sin, but so is not fully exploiting an idea. Best times? It's up to you. Early morning, in the evening when you've settled in for the night, or possibly during a long lunch break when you're peaceful and by yourself.

2. *Develop your idea.* Comfortable? Now that you're relaxed, let's start the visualization process. At this early stage, all you've got is an idea. You're excited about it, it's new, but it has to be developed. During the development phase get a firm grip on your idea by describing the vague dimensions using numbered steps. On a piece of paper, number the major points or factors of your idea. It may have five points, or as many as ten or twenty. The numbered points pave the way for the next step.

3. *Let it become a vague picture.* Hold on to that pencil and paper; you'll need it. With numbered dimensions of your idea in front of you, construct a vague picture of your idea. You can do it mentally, but it's a lot easier if you outline your idea on paper. With each step you're gathering more information, giving you greater options for development. At this point, don't be upset if you can't get a firm handle on your idea. You're not supposed to. It's still unclear, and predictably cloudy.

If you're working out the details for a new machine tool, for example, at this stage all you can expect is a bare sketch outlining the development of your idea and a good indication of where you're going to go from here.

This is the last of the inactive phases. With the next step, you're going to move into a more aggressive phase, taking your idea further along.

4. *See and feel details.* As we said, dimensions outlined in previous steps are going to move from an inanimate to an animate stage. With information already gathered, we're going to color in the spaces, connect the lines, and make our cloudy picture strong, real, and relatable. From an outline phase, we're going to add details and specific dimensions. As an example, think of

yourself as a marketing expert who's fashioned a unique marketing program for a new video game that's going to capture the under-18 set. In the prior stage, all you had was a vague outline for your plan. Now it's crystallized and fleshed out. You've considered the pros and cons, you've analyzed your idea from every conceivable angle. You've thought about the competition and how they'll rush the market with similar products. To prevent any mishaps, you've concocted a counter plan to convince wholesalers and customers alike that your plan is the best on the market. At this advanced stage you're ready to move to the next phase and cope with criticism, opposition, and problems.

5. *Talk to your characters.* Think of moving from stage 3 to stage 4 as the transition from a silent to a talking film.

As we move from one step to another, we have more involvement, until we get to a point where we almost mirror the real life situation. In this phase, we're going to drop the appropriate characters into our homemade visualization drama. Let's pick up our marketing-expert anecdote and find out what happens. As we said, you've considered all aspects of the problem. At this point you round out the visualization process by putting in all the right people, such as your supervisor, executive vice president, and president of the company, as well as support characters, distributors, wholesalers, and a couple of formidable retail chain execs. Each one of these characters is talking to you. Hopefully, you'll be astute enough not to inject characters who will merely flatter and pump up your ego. That's self-defeating. More realistically, put in all the key characters who will both support and criticize your work. This way you can address yourself to every contingency and iron out any wrinkles missed along the way.

During this most important phase, I encourage *interaction*. Don't just think up objections raised by critics and logical answers to follow. Play different parts and get involved with the action. Answer your opponents, argue with them. You'll be surprised at the confidence you'll gain by actually carrying on a conversation with yourself. By engaging in this little exercise you may even pick up errors and reasoning, which can easily be corrected. What you're actually doing by actively interacting with key characters in your visualization drama is brainstorming by yourself. Questions and problems are offered by critics, and you're refuting them and presenting logical arguments in rebuttal. Once you've satisfied all your opponents and critics, and answerd all questions raised by superiors, move on to the final step.

6. *Believe in your visualized idea.* Finally, believe in and have faith in the visualization process. While it can be a lot of fun, it is the fartherst thing from a meaningless game. If you take it seriously and believe in your powers, it can lead to the development and ultimate realization of your idea.

A Kansas City—based architect uses visualization all the time. He told me he rarely sees anything in a three-dimensional form in the beginning. "My ideas start in my head and they're like faint lines drawn with a light pencil," he begins. "There is no real shape to them, only a hint of structure. Something is happening and I'm not really sure where it will go. I carry the idea around with me and the more I think about it and visualize it, the larger and more detailed it becomes. The lines become stronger, darker, and more recognizable. If I stay with it everything is eventually filled in. Before long, that three-dimensional shape has walls, structure, and an identity all its own."

A sales-promotion manager of a large department store said all his good ideas develop by the process of visualization. "An idea for a new clothing or cosmetic line often occurs to me as I'm walking from one end of the store to the other," he says. "The process is so fast, I'm barely conscious of it. The idea whips through my head and disappears just as fast. Thankfully, many of these ideas return when appropriately triggered. If it's a point-of-purchase display for a new cosmetic line it returns again when I'm walking past the cosmetic counters. Second time around, I make it a point to focus on the idea long enough to begin the process of visualization. That's how many of my ideas develop and are eventually realized."

While each of us experiences visualization differently, the process assumes familiar patterns. First, as the sales-promotion manager said, an idea appears, disappears, and then reappears before you're able to latch on to it and visualize it clearly.

Next, the shape of the idea moves from a flimsy, barely visible stage to a solid, substantial three-dimensional form. And finally, the process is almost always a private one. Most people who rely on visualization as a creative tool keep it to themselves. The idea lingers in our consciousness and is kept alive by constantly developing it until it is recognizable.

A stock broker compares his good ideas to tasty bits of candy that he keeps tucked away in the back of his mouth. "I savor those ideas and develop them by visualizing them to a point where I can act on them," he says. "Very often I need a workable investment strategy in order to interest clients in a speculative stock. First the idea occurs to me and if it has any potential at all, I bat it around in my head until I know what to do with it."

Keep in mind that just as ideas are kindled in the process of visualization, they're also aborted by their creators for lack of potential. This is why we fashioned a six-step visualization process. By working on your idea in successive stages, you're taking it on a trial run. You're testing it, and working it out in your mind and on paper to see if it can fly by itself. This is why it's important not to rush the process along. Often you won't get past step 2 or 3. If things aren't falling into place, and you can't find missing parts and links, it's time either to alter your idea or possibly to abandon it. Or, as often happens, your idea may take an interesting turn in the process of visualization, and you wind up with something totally different, better than the idea you originally started with. The key to it all is not to have expectations. Don't rush and don't get discouraged if things don't work out as planned. Go with it, and see where it leads. If you're patient and diligent, you won't be disappointed. No matter what happens, you've used your creativity and learned a lot in the bargain.

CHAPTER 6
CONSTRUCT
REALISTIC
FANTASIES

Closely allied to visualization is *fantasy*, the free flight of thoughts, ideas, and dreams. In the process of visualization, you're consciously constructing tangible forms and shapes based upon information taken from the real world. When fantasizing, you're entering a new world where more daring ideas surface and disturb your thought processes.

In the preceding section, our architect used visualization to start the creative process. Visualization put the creative wheels in motion. It allowed him to see forms and shapes that would later be developed and ultimately realized. But he also has fantasies, which play an important role in augmenting his creativity. To illustrate, just before he dozes off to sleep, his mind zooms off into the atmosphere where he sees fantastic architectural structures that point to new horizons in design and use of imaginative materials. Where visualization helped him create realizable structures, fantasy takes him to new frontiers, where the possible and impossible merge. He sees futuristic homes, experimental structures that have never been designed before. Part of his fantasies are remote and unobtainable, while others can be realized if developed logically. The difficult part is separating the real and unreal elements and finding that common denominator that points to the initial stages of creativity. Once you're able to accomplish that, the fantasy can be harnessed, paving the way for the visualization of thoughts.

All of us have fantasies. Some fantasize more than others, and others never allow these secret thoughts to surface. These days, fantasies are getting a good deal of attention, with psychiatrists and psychologists insisting we should all get in touch with our innermost fantasies in order to lead more fulfilling lives. Take a look at some of the covers of popular consumer magazines, and you're bound to see some enticing stories on sexual fantasies and how great they are for getting in touch with your innermost thoughts. After you separate fact from fiction, and sensationalism from cold reality, there is a good deal of truth to much of what is written about fantasies.

Fantasies can be very valuable. The trick, however, is knowing how to harness them. Let's take a closer look at fantasies and the role they play in our lives and careers. Fantasies can be separated into two broad categories: realistic and unrealistic fantasies. First, unrealistic fantasies.

An *unrealistic* fantasy can be compared to a favorite movie running through your mind. The movie appeals to you, you identify with the action, yet it bears little connection to your life. Nevertheless, the characters and plot turn you on to the point where you allow your mind to wallow in these temporary breaks from reality.

A friend of mine falls into the above category. A computer science professor, he has a passion for Clint Eastwood films. He's seen every film the actor made at least once—favorites, three and four times. Why? My friend is the first to admit Eastwood is no Olivier, O'Toole, or Richardson, yet the actor triggers something inside him that constantly brings him back for more. This erudite professor explains: "I guess you'd call it positive identification. Eastwood is tough, sullen, and always victorious. He looks good and he always gets the girl. He's the quintessential macho hero. Aside from enjoying the brawl and fight scenes and the impossible situations, part of me wants to be just like Clint Eastwood. It could never happen, but it's great fun letting my imagination run wild every so often."

There is nothing unusual about my friend. Many of us have similar fantasies. We empathize with film and television stars, athletes, rock stars, and the super rich. They lead enviable lives, they're in the limelight, they're rich and successful, and in our fantasies we want to be just like them.

Several years ago, *The Millionaire* was a successful television series. In it a philanthropic millionaire gave away millions of dollars to worthy people who could make good use of it. The lucky person could do whatever he wanted with the money as long as he didn't reveal its source. A common fantasy at the time involved a well-dressed gentleman knocking on someone's door and handing over an envelope containing a cashier's check for $1 million.

The above fantasies are fun to think about. They're like tasty bits of chocolate that are tucked away in the back of our mouths to be savored and enjoyed right down to the last sweet morsel. As fantastic as they are, they never will see the light of day. They serve no other purpose but to entertain and amuse.

An unrealistic fantasy is weighted down by improbable and unreal elements. Take the 55-year-old retailer who fantasizes about becoming president, the 34-year-old auto salesman who envisions himself an Olympic bike racer, or the accountant who fantasizes about discovering a cure for cancer. They're all unrealistic fantasies. It's important to see them for what they are. They're like whipped-cream topping on a cake. The whipped cream has no real nutritional value and the pleasure derived from eating it is short-lived.

Realistic fantasies, on the other hand, fall into a more tangible realm. If developed, they can serve as catalysts in the creative process. Imagine the following realistic fantasies. A corporate attorney fantasizes about owning a fleet of tankers; a telephone company switching technician fantasizes about becoming a systems analyst; a lab assistant wishes he could become a well-known surgeon; or an electronics technician fantasizes about designing a new compact computer. What makes these fantasies realistic? The fact that they contain seeds of truth that could, if properly nurtured, become real.

An enterprising corporate attorney could make a number of clever business maneuvers that lead to owning a fleet of tankers; a telephone switching technician has the mechanical aptitude to become a systems analyst; it may take a number of years, but it's not impossible for a lab assistant to go back to school and prepare to be a surgeon; or, similarly, for an electronics technician to design a compact computer.

It's just a question of getting in touch with that fantasy, looking at it critically and separating its real and unreal parts. If it's top-heavy in realistic elements, it stands a good chance of coming true and, conversely, if it's weighted down in unrealistic elements, it's doomed to be nothing more than a pleasant interlude.

Let's get in touch with our fantasies and see if they can be applied to our jobs. Imagine you're carrying around a great sales, computer, instrument, or information idea that has you baffled. You're frustrated. You'd give anything to see it get off the ground. The idea is waiting for a gentle shove so that it can be developed further and eventually realized.

Start by making sure your fantasies are realistic and then ask yourself the following questions:

1. Do I have the necessary career qualifications to make the fantasy come true?
2. Can the fantasy be easily connected and applied to my work setting?

If the answer is yes to both of the above questions, let's proceed and work on constructing our fantasies. Just as we carved the visualization process in the previous chapter into a number of parts, we're going to apply a similar method to our fantasies. The process of constructing fantasies can be broken down into the following seven-stage process:

1. Relax
2. Outline your fantasy
3. Harness your imagination
4. Write your fantasy down
5. Clarify it
6. Visualize it
7. Revise it

1. *Relax.* You can have a fantasy any time or place. You can have

one while walking down a city street, or while sitting in a crowded subway car. Like visualization, the ideal time is when you're relaxed and comfortable. It's when you're in no rush to get somewhere, when you have time to ponder your thoughts. After dinner, while reading or watching television, or just before dozing off to sleep are ideal times to build fantasies. During these off-moments, you can devote time to thinking and developing your ideas. You no longer have to contend with the tensions and problems you face all day long.

2. *Outline your fantasy*. In this early stage, you're going to get in touch with your fantasy. Think of yourself as a carpenter building the foundation of a house. The structure of the house is being erected, the support beams are almost in place. You're going to do the same thing with your fantasy. You're gathering the cement, brick, steel, and wood beams, everything needed to build a sturdy realistic fantasy that will see the light of day. Imagine you're low person on the corporate totem pole. You're a junior executive, and you've only been with the company six months. But you have dreams, big dreams. You see yourself rising through the ranks, eventually becoming president of the company. What's more, you see yourself devising cost-effective systems and adopting sophisticated telecommunications systems, all helping to make your company a leader in its field.

While the general fantasy seems clear, the details have to be systematically worked out. In this phase, you're going to outline the bare details of your fantasy. With a compass, draw a circle. Start from the top of the circle and outline a path for yourself. In this early stage, don't rack your brains searching for details and formulas. All that's needed is a vague roadmap to point you in the right direction. This is why I like the circle. To give yourself a clear sense of direction, at different points on the circle add goals and comments. Once completed, move to the next stage where you're going to gather more material, thus more clearly defining your fantasy.

3. *Harness your imagination*. You know where you're going, the path is outlined for you. But you've got a long way to go. What's more, you need details, information. More specifically, you need a unique touch, an approach that is going to hurdle you to the very top of the corporate heap. Don't be naive, you're not the only one who fantasizes about cornering the top executive position. Every other junior exec worth his salt also has eyes riveted on the executive suite. However, you realize you can do it, if you

have what it takes. And what it takes is uniqueness, something special. In short, imagination, that which distinguishes you from everyone else. This is a thinking stage, where you're going to devise strategies, techniques, and mind-boggling formulas that will make you stand out. Once they take shape, you're ready to move on to the next phase.

4. *Write your fantasy down.* Now you're cooking. The thoughts are rocketing through your head faster than the speed of sound. You can hardly keep track of all the brilliant imaginative strategies that are bouncing about your brain. Your head is throbbing, pulsating with excitement. Before any of it escapes you, grab a pencil and write everything down. Don't worry about precision and accuracy. Just get it down on paper. In the next stage, you'll clean up the language and shape it further. Don't rush to the next stage until you've got everything down on paper. Once you've emptied your mind, proceed.

5. *Clarify it.* This is an easy stage. Go back to the scribbled fantasy and tighten up the language. Pretend you're a high-paid editor and eliminate excess verbiage. Your job is to clarify the fantasy by removing extraneous information. Trim it to skin and bones so only facts are left. You're going to feel terrific when you finish. You'll feel as if you exercised for a solid thirty minutes and knocked off five pounds in the process. Finished? Let's move on to a more active stage.

6. *Visualize it.* I don't have to tell you what visualization is all about. Now that your fantasy is crystal clear, it's time to breathe life into it by visualizing it in all its exciting details. The fantasy is no longer abstract; it's lifelike and real and, through the process of visualization outlined earlier, you can see and feel yourself moving through the various stages. You're aggressively climbing the corporate ladder, rung after rung, creating and devising imaginative strategies along the way, till you've arrived at your ultimate plateau and victory. As an added precaution, however, we've added one last stage.

7. *Revise it.* Why not be as accurate as possible? It's never too late to refine and smooth out rough edges. After coming this far, you may discover that your fantasy needs more work. This is the time to do it. If you feel you have to back up a couple of steps in order to make changes, by all means do it. Don't compromise. Don't forget, your goal is to make a realistic fantasy come true. It can be done—if you're patient, and willing to take the time to make it work.

Once a realistic fantasy is identified and expanded upon, it can be tied to conquerable goals. Our fantasy is no longer a never-to-be-realized wish, but a logical thought that can be translated into reality.

If you can profit from your fantasies, there is no reason why you can't go on and tap your dreams as well. You'll soon see that dreams can be used for developing ideas as well as for problem solving.

CHAPTER 7
PROGRAM
YOUR DREAMS

Since Freud wrote *The Interpretation of Dreams*, hundreds of books have been written about dreams. In spite of all the literature on the subject, dreams will still remain a mystery to most of us.

It's great fun playing amateur psychoanalyst, trying to patch together bits and pieces of seemingly irrelevant dream sequences in order to find a common theme. Easier said than done. Nevertheless, dreams are fascinating and, without knowing the first thing about Freudian symbolism, they can provide an interesting roadmap to your psyche and even help augment your creativity.

Explore the history texts and you'll find fascinating examples of visionary dreams. Allusions to dreams were an integral part of the New Testament, especially the vision to Joseph concerning the birth of Jesus and later the dream that warned him to flee Egypt.

The night before Waterloo, Napoleon was reported to have dreamed of seeing a black cat cross from one army to the other and then of his own army being cut to pieces. If Napoleon had heeded this frightening dream, the course of history would have been changed.

Just before his death, Abraham Lincoln supposedly dreamed about a soldier guarding a coffin in the White House. When asked who had died, he was told that it was the President. And it was a dream that led Hannibal to make his march across the Alps, Alexander the Great to conquer Tyre, and the Moorish leader ibn-Ziyad to begin the conquest of Spain.

Dreams have also been cited as the source for major breakthroughs in science and the arts. A classic story revolves around Isaac Singer, the inventor of the sewing machine. Singer supposedly saw the design for the special harpoon-shaped needle during a dream.

The German chemist Friedrich Kekule worked for years trying to solve the structure of benzene. After a dream in which he saw six snakes biting each other's tails in a circle, he interpreted it as a hexagon—and the chemical structure for benzene.

And critical scenes in *Dr. Jekyll and Mr. Hyde* were credited by author Robert Louis Stevenson to vivid dreams he experienced during a period while grappling with difficult passages.

Formidable examples can be enumerated telling how inventors, scientists, authors, and leaders were shaken, moved, or profited by dreams. The crucial question is how can we benefit from a dream, how can we use a dream as a launching pad for a creative idea. Many people may dream a solution without recognizing it. For instance, the chemist who interpreted the six snakes correctly as being symbols for the shape of a hexagon might have seen them only as snakes. There is often a degree of symbolism and mystery about the images in dreams that requires interpretation by the dreamer.

Another problem is that we often forget the content of our dreams as soon as we awaken. While the average person has between five and six dreams a night, he's lucky if he recalls one well. In a laboratory setting, subjects have been awakened periodically during dream periods, and they have remembered as many as a dozen in a single night.

We face two problems: how to use dreams to augment creativity and how to increase dream recall. First, tips on how to use dreams to feed the creative process.

Some people have been more successful at this than others, but sleep researchers tell us that we can program our dreams to help us solve problems. One such technique was developed by Gayle Delaney, Ph.D., a California psychologist. According to Dr. Delaney, dreams can be used to help solve problems. Our dreams, says Dr. Delaney, are not merely something we receive but, instead, they are something we create in order to get a message across to our waking selves. In her book, *Living Your Dreams*, and in her private practice, she teaches people how to make their dreams a part of their everyday awareness and a source of insight into their waking lives.

Imagine walking around all day with a great idea. You came up with the germ of something you can't wait to develop and your imagination is fired. However, you're blocked and you can't seem to get past the idea stage. The idea is bouncing about your brain and you're not quite sure how to proceed. What next? All it takes is some clever programming and the right conditions, and you stand a good chance of finding some answers in your dreams.

Using a technique called dream incubation, Dr. Delaney says you can go to sleep in the evening and request a dream that will solve a specific problem. This is a process, she says, that has been used since ancient times. Here's how to make it work.

1. *Start with a clear and precise question that will ultimately give way to an answer.* "When you go to bed and turn out the lights," explains Dr. Delaney, "simply repeat the question to yourself over and over again. If your mind starts to wander, keep coming back to the question. The repetition will not allow you to worry about the problem because it forces you to keep your attention on the question. It's also like counting sheep and will help put you to sleep. You should wake up in the morning with an idea from your dream about how to solve your problem."

2. *As you awaken with the idea, write it down immediately.* If you don't complete this important step, you may forget the dream and your efforts will be in vain. Often the answer to your question will be obvious in your dream; sometimes it will not. If not, Dr. Delaney suggests you think about the dream—specifically, the setting, the objects in the dream, and anything else that stands out about it. By thinking of the dream as a parable and its

parts as a metaphor, you should be able to determine the message your sleep conscious was trying to get across to your waking conscious.

What dream researchers are still puzzling over is why we can solve problems in our dreams that we can't solve in our waking state. Answers aren't apparent yet they've discovered that in a dream state people tend to be more creative, objective, and insightful about their conditions than they are in the waking state. The dream state also seems to provide access to subliminal information not available in the waking state.

Finally, some tips on increasing dream recall. According to Chicago sleep researcher R. Rosalind Cartwright, the ability to recall dreams is related to how and why we wake up. Interestingly, we are more inclined to remember dreams on a weekend than during the week because we have the time and interest to try and shift back to catch the dream we are just experiencing. During the week, most people move immediately into their morning routine and never backtrack to the dream stage.

To encourage dream recall, remember the following pointers:

1. Before going to sleep, coach yourself by saying several times that you will remember your dreams.
2. Go to sleep relaxed and tension-free, and try to get enough rest.
3. Set your alarm at two-hour intervals in order to catch yourself in the middle of a dream.

The above methods have been successful with some and unsuccessful with others. Whether you actually use your dreams to aid creativity, you lose nothing by trying. If nothing else, the quiet response of the late night hours is an excellent time for thinking, and for introspection.

CHAPTER 8
RESEARCH
YOUR IDEA
THOROUGHLY

There are three kinds of ideas: ideas that are unique (the one-of-a-kind variety), ideas that are variations of something already on the market, and, finally, ideas that have already been developed and exploited. It's up to you to determine in which category your idea belongs.

This is where careful, painstaking research comes in. While you may think you have the widget to beat all widgets, the quintessential product that will put everyone else out of business, don't be foolish and think no one has done it before. You may discover that, a decade earlier, an almost identical product was developed in London. It's disappointing, but these are facts of life that we all have to face whether we like it or not.

It's important that you carefully research your idea in its early stages before you invest a great deal of time and energy in your project. The computer science engineer who develops a new microprocessor cannot risk making the assumption that one hasn't been invented. And since every major industrial power is developing its own technology, his research has to extend way beyond the borders of his own country. A Japanese, German, French, or Australian engineer may have developed a similar product. Take the fashion designer who has what she thinks is a new synthetic fiber that could knock polyester off the market. Having spent over twenty-five years in the field, she's almost positive nothing like it exists. *Almost* is not good enough, however. If she's current with developments in her field, she's probably right. Nevertheless, she still has to go through the necessary steps and make sure she is the first and only inventor of the new synthetic fiber.

Even within companies, new ideas and concepts have to be carefully researched to make sure no duplication exists. If you happen to be working for a multinational company with divisions and subsidiaries all over the world, your research may take longer than expected.

Nobody enjoys spending weeks, even months, researching an idea. But think of it as a necessary investment of your time. If you believe in your idea, you have no choice but to do everything in your power to make sure it sees the light of day.

You're not to throw in the towel on learning someone else has explored your idea. That's the easy way out. A cynical writer acquaintance told me there is no such thing as an original idea. "It's all been done before," he sneered. "It's just a question of coming up with a new approach to an old problem." I don't agree with him totally, but there is some truth in what he says. While a good part of a person's or even a country's creative output is a restatement, elaboration, or embellishment of previous efforts, there are, however, new ideas, discoveries, and concepts born every year.

So in the process of researching your idea, it's very likely that you'll stumble on someone who has done work on your project. This is not to be taken as defeat. Before you have all the information, don't assume that all your hard work has been in vain. Yes, it's possible that someone in another state or country has done exactly what you have done. However, it's also likely that the researcher (or researchers) approached the problem differently and came to different conclusions.

Learn to benefit from the work of others. By discovering that someone else has explored your area, chances are excellent that you'll wind up learning more, thus making your contribution all the more valuable.

Few scientists, for example, work in total isolation. Scientific exploration is based upon systematically analyzing others' work so progress can be made. The scientific community is large and spread out all over the world, yet scientists make it a point to keep up with developments in the field. Through periodicals or the university circuit or more directly by corresponding with one another, they keep all their channels open in order to absorb as much information as they can. This paves the way for scientific discovery.

In an essay on scientific creativity (North-Holland Publishing Company, Amsterdam), Nobel Prize winner Dr. Willard F. Libby writes, "Scientific creativity is scientific discovery through scientific research. It is the essence of science." And in discussing a scientist's work, he says, "He [the scientist] must be willing and ready to discard his own theories in the face of observation and though he is not required to rejoice at such a development, he must take it as scientific progress and must try to make a new or modified theory to fit the more completely enlightened situation."

We can all learn something from the scientific approach. More often than not, in the process of researching others' contributions, new ideas and thoughts are triggered. All of a sudden, new approaches appear before you. Prior to your research, you mistakenly thought there was only one way to attack the problem. But in the process of investigating the subject, you were delighted to discover that a number of prominent people in your field also probed the issue using an altogether fresh approach.

A marketing analyst, for example, was troubled about a new concept he was trying to puzzle out. He took it so far and was unable to proceed further. Instead of abandoning the project, he had enough sense to put his work aside in order to find out if any colleagues had explored this area. To his surprise, he learned that work had been done in an allied field, thus pointing him in the right direction. Now he could proceed to the next step and develop his idea further.

Despite all those romantic Hollywood epics showing writers and artists working in total seclusion miles from civilization, the truth is that most creators maintain some contact with the outside world, or at least with their professional, crafts, or artistic community. In order to do first-rate work and keep up with state-of-the-art developments, one technician or engineer has to know what others are doing. The same goes for individuals working in any field you care to mention. While parts of the creative process take place in isolation, at some point (or points) the creator has to reach out to discover what others have done.

In researching an idea, keep the following pointers in mind:

1. *Beforehand, plan a research campaign or strategy.* It should answer the following questions:

a. What is it you're looking for?
b. What do you plan on doing with the information once you find it?

2. *Spread your research over a broad front.* Don't rely on one library; use several. Beyond published books and periodicals, there are many other sources of information: trade associations, scientific groups and organizations, private think tanks, government agencies, and so on.

3. *Don't confine yourself to just one central idea.* Search for information in related or allied fields. You'll be surprised at what you'll discover.

4. *Consider contacting experts or authorities in your field.* Play detective and find them. An industry association, for one, may be happy to help you out. If the person you're looking for has written one or several books, write to the publisher, who in turn will forward your letter to the author. It may take time, but it's worth the effort.

5. *Make sure your research is orderly and systematic.* Keep files, date material, and take clear, concise notes so you avoid repetition and error.

CHAPTER 9
FIND A
ROLE MODEL

Just as it's vital to study and follow the work of others and keep current with developments in your field, it's equally important to have creative role models to emulate.

Children as well as adults need role models. The important difference between a child's role model and an adult's is that the child's role model is usually an integral part of the child's fantasy world, whereas the adult's model serves a more practical end. Some children dream of growing up and being just like their favorite football, basketball, or baseball players. Other children dream of becoming astronauts, famous heart surgeons, and even finding cures for life-threatening diseases. Most children outgrow their fantasies, and then again a tiny percentage actually make them come true.

As we mature, we give up our models and idols and settle down to the realities of earning a living and surviving. Certainly, the everyday realities can't be avoided, yet it's important to never lose sight of the role models that count, the ones we can learn from, who help us get better at whatever we do.

A young idealistic poet told me that everyone should have a role model or idol to look up to. "The problem with so many people is they're so ready to settle for mediocrity," he said. "The only way a person can hone his craft is by working with someone better than himself." I agree. Interestingly, that premise is the basis and rationale for our apprenticeship system. The apprenticeship system is a carefully worked-out program whereby young, aspiring craftspeople learn to become master craftspeople. A thorough way to accomplish that end is by assisting journeymen workers (experienced craftspeople) for a specific period of time. Depending upon the trade, it could take anywhere from three to five years to learn enough to go out and earn a living. A few more years of working on their own and they will be able to claim journeyman status.

Apprenticeship programs still exist, although they're quickly losing ground to more formalized learning programs. Yet the concept is still sound and bears emulating. Look back upon history and you'll see that every great person had someone he looked up to and emulated.

Let's take our poet's cue and find a creative role model to emulate. First, let's identify qualities this person should have.

1. Outstanding in field; impressive credentials
2. Aggressive, outspoken, articulate
3. Positive attitude toward career; strives for conquest, victory, fulfillment

Where can this person be found?

1. May be within your organization
2. May be with another company or organization
3. May be retired or deceased
4. May be an outspoken force or authority in your field or industry

It's not essential that you meet this person. What *is* important is that the image and reputation of the role model is powerful enough to inspire and motivate you. He's overcome incredible odds, he's distinguished himself by doing unusual, innovative work. He's broken new ground, and within a relatively short period of time he's built a reputation as a leader and authority in his field. You want to be just like him.

However, if you can meet the person, all the better. You have the opportunity to ply him with questions and find out firsthand how he got where he is. If a meeting can be arranged, here are some questions you might want to ask him.

- How long have you worked in the field?
- What strategies and methods did you use to achieve your goals?
- Did you have a goal plan? How detailed was it, and did you adjust it as you went along?
- How did you cope with competition?
- What did you do that was unique?
- Are there any secrets to success? What useful tips would you pass on to others?
- What do you ultimately hope to achieve?

The above questions are only a working guide. I'm sure you can think of many more that are relevant to your particular situation. The idea is to ask questions you can profit from and apply to yourself. Your goal is to gather valuable information so you too can be an outstanding performer in your field.

You don't have to confine yourself to one role model. You may have two or more, each for different reasons. One person may be an outstanding leader in one segment of your field, the other in another segment of your field. If your goal is to bridge divergent, yet connected career sectors, having two role models makes a lot of sense. For instance, if you're hellbent on rising to the top of your advertising agency and you possess both writing and selling skills, consider having a top-flight copywriter to look up to who can inspire you to greater creative heights, as well as a prominent account executive who's built an impressive sales record.

As you advance in your job, you may find that you've overtaken your role model. What now? Are you finally free of role models once and for all? Absolutely not. If you're still working toward that elusive goal of perfection, find another role model to look up to. I doubt if you've learned everything there is to know about your field. There is still ground to cover. Don't be content to rest on your laurels. Find that special role model who dominates your field so you can learn everything he knows and one day be as great or greater than he is. It can be done, if you believe in your abilities and powers.

Now you can understand why journalists routinely ask their subjects questions like: "Who was your model?" Or, "Who inspired you?" Without fail, the questions trigger a warm response where the interviewee gushes about the person or individuals who inspired him and helped him realize his goals.

Think about your own work situation and the people who taught you the ropes. Step aside and evaluate them objectively. Are they the best at what they do? Are you profiting from the relationship, or could you have done better? Or maybe you've absorbed all they can teach and it's time to move on.

Answer the above questions and decide on an appropriate course of action. Clearly, we need others to teach us in order that we can pick up the slack and carry on where they left off. If we are to be better than our mentors, it's crucial that we get the very best instruction we can.

CHAPTER 10
LISTEN
ACTIVELY

Listen? you say. "That's easy. I listen to people all day long. I listen to my kids and husband at home and when I'm at work, I listen to my co-workers and boss. How can I get through a day *without* listening to people?"

Easily. Millions do it. Many of us think we're listening when in fact all we're doing is playing out a life drama that was taught to us as children. You must have heard your parents tell you to listen quietly and respectfully when others speak. That means not interrupting until the other person is finished and waiting for the right moment to express an opinion. That's about as far as it went.

What we weren't told was *how* to listen. Listening isn't just being quiet when someone else speaks. You're not really listening, you're only a respectful sounding board. Words are flung at you and maybe every other word hits its mark. Unknowingly, we've become expert at affecting the right expression and coming back with the expected responses when people talk to us. We nod our heads, laugh, sigh, and play our roles to the hilt. Consider how many great ideas, plans for new products, selling or marketing strategies are lost at staff meetings and in the course of routine conversations because of ineffectual listening.

Serious listening is something else entirely. It means absorbing what another person is saying. It involves thought, concentration, and critical appraisal. Knowing how to listen requires work and energy. Serious listening implies a give-and-take relationship. It's not something learned overnight. It takes years to master. However, it's well worth the effort because active listeners retain more information and are more creative in their work. By retaining vast quantities of information, they have the wherewithal to harness their creative energy more effectively.

As a young reporter, I learned the hard way. With a reporter's notebook and a leaky ballpoint pen, I was daily faced with the nerve-racking task of getting enough information to put together a coherent story. Easier said than done. It meant approaching a situation relaxed, with an open mind, ready to digest information. An experienced reporter develops this technique to a fine art. He confronts his subject, asks pointed questions, maintains eye contact at all times, and then listens intently to answers so he can record them quickly, succinctly, and accurately.

A novice reporter, on the other hand, often approaches his subject with trepidation, an obvious handicap. If he's prepared, he manages to ask all the right questions. However, he's often so concerned with making a good impression, and coming off like a seasoned investigative reporter, that he almost doesn't hear the answers to his questions. The result is confusion and often chaos. Instead of hearing complete thoughts and recording feelings, impressions, and emotions, he picks up bits and pieces of information. Facts are in no particular order; accuracy is questionable.

The tough part comes when our young reporter sits down at the typewriter to bang out his story. Now he faces problems he wasn't prepared for. What might take an experienced reporter an hour and a half to accomplish takes our young friend two and possibly three times as much time. All the rambling, unsubstantiated facts have to be rechecked before he can put the story together.

It's all part of the learning process, and most reporters go through it to a greater or lesser extent. The root of the young reporter's problem stems from an inability to listen to and hear what others are saying. Through trial and error, he hones his craft and in the process becomes a more effective and more creative reporter. Skills mastered in hearing and recording information spill over to his social life as well. Relationships become easier, more meaningful, and a lot more beneficial.

The act of listening in a conversation can be compared to a relaxed game of catch. You throw the ball to someone, and he tosses it back to you. The game may start off a little awkwardly, but before you know it, it progresses smoothly and effortlessly. If you're sustaining the game over a period of time there's an obvious rhythm to your motions. A similar process takes place while listening. You express a thought (or thoughts) to someone, the other person quickly records the information, makes a judgment, and then answers your questions, renders an opinion, or possibly disagrees with what you said, thus fueling you for another reply. Like the game of catch, a conversation proceeds with a slow, progressive rhythm.

Learning to listen actively takes time. It's analogous to speed reading. Just because you take a course in speed reading doesn't mean you're an expert speed reader. You've been taught speed reading techniques, now you have to practice them until they are part of you. The same rationale applies to listening.

The active listener retains eighty-five percent to one hundred percent of the information he hears. The average person retains somewhere between fifty and sixty-five percent of what he hears. Polite, ineffectual listeners barely retain fifty percent of what is said.

Let's sharpen our listening powers with the following exercises:

Exercise #1

Tape fifteen-minute radio segments and play them back to yourself. On a piece of paper, write down all the information you retained. Don't be upset if you remember very little the first time. Remember, listening is a skill that has to be developed. And the only way to accomplish that is by working at it. The first time you may be upset to discover you retained about forty percent of the material. Do it again, but this time relax. A poor technique is hanging onto individual words. In the end, all you'll retain is small particles of information. Instead, listen for ideas, concepts, thoughts. The more listening you do, the better you'll retain important facts and ideas.

After doing this exercise, give yourself some recuperation time before going at it again. Or have several fifteen-minute segments that you can listen to repeatedly to test your retentive powers.

Initially, tape light material. Don't start off taping a lecture on nuclear physics, or a philosophical/religious discussion on the meaning of life. Instead, tape a talk show on new diet fads, tips on rearing children, news broadcasts, and so on. Tape information that you can relate to and that is fairly easy to absorb.

After you get really good at remembering fifteen-minute tape segments and you're retaining better than eighty to eighty-five percent of what you hear, go on to more daring exercises. Try taping a twenty- or thirty-minute program and see how much you remember.

Exercise #2

If you don't have a tape recorder, try remembering conversations. Don't confine yourself to business conversations, but think of conversations at home with your family, even conversations you happen to overhear. Do this every chance you get, and it won't be long before you develop special powers. You'll be delighted to learn that you hear things that elude others. The result is more food for thought. Instead of having little chunks of information circulating in your brain, your mind will become a vast storehouse of information. You'll have the resources to develop ideas, concepts, and the background information to problem-solve more efficiently.

Exercise #3

Practice remembering names. Most people have trouble remembering names. Did you ever go to a party, meet fifteen new
people in the space of thirty seconds, and, as soon as the last
name is mentioned, forget all of them. It happens to everyone.
The next time you're in a situation like this, business or social,
try hard to remember the names of the people you meet.

Crackerjack salespeople work hard to develop this skill early
in their careers. They're constantly meeting new people and, if
they hope to generate new business, they've discovered that it
helps to remember people's names. As a regional sales manager
of a large pharmaceutical firm put it, "A real pro never forgets a
name. He'll meet someone he hasn't seen in a year and he'll
remember the name immediately. That's talent." More than
talent, it's a skill anyone can develop if they work at it.

Try one of these exercises. Open yourself up to broader listening experiences. Turn your ears into tape recorders and your
mind into a computer bank. You'll be amazed at the number of
creative ideas this will generate.

CHAPTER 11
READ!
READ!
READ!

Just as the creative person must be an active listener, he must also be an active reader. He must read everything he can get his hands on and make it his business to retain most of it. As a favorite English professor used to say, "The involved reader has an insatiable appetite for knowledge. He's a bottomless pit who never tires of amassing, storing, and eventually using the information he retrieves."

Sadly, though, most of us read little. The average person barely gets through the daily newspaper. Typically, most people read what interests them, be it sports, business, or general news, and discard the paper. A veteran journalist told me the average reader barely reads twenty-five percent of a Sunday edition, the fattest edition of the week.

Just as listening can heighten and expand your creative powers, both on and off the job, reading can achieve similar results. First, open yourself up to the smorgasbord of exciting literature out there. You'd be surprised at what it can do for you. Not only will it inspire you, but it will motivate you to read more, and expand your information base. The end result is, you guessed it, new sources of ideas, new problem-solving techniques; hence, a thousand and one avenues to expand upon and increase your on-the-job creativity.

Not only does the average person not read that much, he's also not aware of the wealth of information out there. Beyond newsstand magazines and newspapers, and books borrowed or bought, consider the following sources of reading material.

1. *Public relations sources.* Under the umbrella heading of public relations, millions of words are expended each year. Large and small companies maintain public relations departments that would be delighted to send you whatever they produce. Their function is to keep the media and public informed regarding developments, discoveries, breakthroughs, product information, you name it. Beyond in-house public relations departments, there are private PR firms that specialize in various types of accounts—cosmetics, chemical, fashion, and so on. There are also industry associations that exist solely to promote a good image for the industry they serve. Think of an industry and there is bound to be an association that will be delighted to send you a truckload of helpful information.

How do you find out where the associations are located? Simple. Fifteen minutes in your local library thumbing through the *Associations Directory* and you'll have the name, address, phone number, and person to contact at each association.

Whatever industry you serve, it pays to keep in touch with your industry association or organization. A simple telephone call or letter will put you on the mailing list, keeping you abreast of developments, news items, and recent appointments. Many of the large associations, such as associations serving the steel, textile, and food industries, publish up-to-the-minute career information. You owe it to yourself to stay on top of developments in your field. Don't wait for a job recruiter or placement manager to tell you a competing firm is opening a $20 million plant in Atlanta offering job opportunities galore. Make it your business to know what's happening in your industry before anyone else.

2. *Government sources.* Do you know our government is a vast

publishing empire, churning out material on a variety of subjects, some of which may be of value to you? And the best part is that most of it is free. I bet you didn't know that. It's not just the media that has access to it, but everyone. The Department of Agriculture, Department of Labor, and the Department of Health and Human Services publish everything from daily press releases, speeches, and news bulletins to four-color magazines.

If you work in the cosmetics/drug industry, does it make sense to be on the mailing list of the Federal Drug Administration (FDA)? If your answer wasn't a vociferous yes, you're either half asleep or just not thinking. By receiving press releases, you'll have a panoramic view of your field, and you'll know what products are being released, which ones are the subject of investigation or controversy, and which ones are being considered for approval.

All government agencies can be found in Washington, D.C., and many of them, such as the Department of Labor, maintain regional offices in major cities throughout the country. The Department of Labor, by the way, is a marvelous source of career information. They publish information on every field you can think of and their yearly edition of the *Occupational Outlook Handbook* provides current statistics on the number of openings in a given field, a career's long-range potential, and broad salary ranges.

3. *Newsletters, special-interest publications.* Newsletters and special-interest magazines are also a fantastic source of information not found in consumer magazines and newspapers. The better newsletters and specialty magazines pride themselves on probing issues in great detail, giving readers information that will help them make important work-related decisions.

Next time you're in your library ask to see one of the several directories listing the variety of newsletters published. Browse through it and jot down the newsletters covering your field. Don't subscribe before seeing it. Ask the publisher to send you promotional material and a sample issue so you can determine whether you can profit from the material. Professional newsletters and magazines are more expensive than consumer magazines, but they're often well worth the price because of the inside, current information they offer.

Now that you have some idea what's out there, consider the following reading strategies:

1. *Vary your reading habits.* Don't confine yourself to reading

work-related magazines, periodicals, and scholarly reports. That can become awfully tedious after a while. Just as an athlete varies his pace, open yourself up to a broad range of reading materials. Get into the habit of reading for different purposes. Spend part of your time reading for information (staying current with developments in your field) and the rest of the time reading for enjoyment. For instance, an Atlanta-based textile designer spends part of his time keeping up with developments in his field and uses his spare time to gobble up biographies, which, he says, fascinate him. "I love reading about other people's lives, especially people who have achieved greatness," he explains. "I enjoy learning how they discovered themselves, overcame obstacles and made their dreams come true. Some biographies I never tire of, such as the biographies of Einstein, Napoleon, and Toscanini. While their goals were different, I uncover similar motivations I can attribute to each man. Each was driven, dedicated, persistent, and had an ego that couldn't be shaken. When I'm discouraged I find that I take enormous sustenance in reading a good biography. In the process of reading about other men's lives, I often learn to adopt and expand upon their problem-solving techniques. In the end, I learn more about tapping my creative powers."

While reading for enjoyment (novel, short story, poetry, etc.) your mind changes currents, relaxes, recharges itself, allowing new energy to be targeted toward gnawing work-related problems.

Make it a point to expand your reading base. It doesn't have to be biographies; it an be anything that interests you, from music, stamps, how-to books, to collecting. Whatever triggers your imagination and fascinates you.

2. *Set reading goals.* If you're an avid reader in wide-ranging subjects, reading goals are not necessary. But if you're an inconsistent reader, establish a minimum reading goal for yourself. Some people set yearly reading goals, possibly ten or fifteen books per year. Better than yearly goals, set monthly goals. Instead of leaving your reading to the last minute, as you're apt to do with a yearly goal, try to read a certain amount each month. Depending upon the time you have available, a realistic goal may be to read two books, and to keep current with the professional magazines in your field. However you do it, work toward incorporating reading rituals into your life scheme.

3. *Find a convenient time and place to read.* What with time

spent traveling to and from work and waiting for people to keep appointments, you can always find fifteen or twenty minutes to do some fast reading. For serious reading, however, find a comfortable time and place. Some people prefer to read late at night, just prior to nodding off to sleep, whereas some early risers find that six to seven in the morning is an ideal time for quiet, undisturbed reading. Whatever time is most convenient, make it your business to read as much as you can within that time period. The place you do your reading is also important. Make sure it's quiet, and that there are no distractions.

4. *Increase your retentive powers.* Just as active listeners remember most of what they hear, an active reader similarly retains most of what he reads. From time to time, test your retentive powers by writing down the nuts and bolts of what you read. This is an exercise often given to teens to help them remember what they read for test-taking purposes. No, you're never too old to play this little game. Try testing your retentive powers with articles from newspapers or magazines. Read a story and jot down the pertinent facts. Don't be discouraged if you remember only forty-five percent of the material. Keep on playing this little game and before you know it you'll stretch your memory and recall better than ninety percent of what you read. Like the active listener, your goal is to focus not on insignificant details but on facts, important thoughts, concepts, opinions, and ideas.

Now that we've strengthened our creative resources by honing our listening and reading skills, let's amass a storehouse of ideas.

CHAPTER 12
ABSORB
IDEAS

Imagine walking through an apple orchard and picking apples from trees. They're right in front of you, accessible, ripe, beckoning to be plucked and eaten. So it is with ideas. All you have to do is open yourself up to them. It was Aristotle who said, "Of things that came to be, some come to be by nature, some by art, some spontaneously."

In weaving the pieces of this book together, I asked a number of people how many viable, work-related ideas they have in a day. The answers ranged from none to several. An accountant said he had only a couple of ideas a day.

"Are you sure?" I asked.

"Absolutely," he returned.

Not believing him, I pursued the subject further, asking him to define idea.

"An *idea* is something that eventually works or can be used to benefit me in some way," he said.

Now I had the picture. But what about all the other ideas that crisscross his mind that he doesn't deem important enough to develop? When I posed that question to him, he responded: "If you look at it that way, I couldn't begin to tell you how many ideas run through my head each day. Maybe twenty-five or thirty. But I only hold on to the ones with potential."

We'll get into the process of banking and storing ideas soon, but, like the accountant, each of us encounters several ideas a day. Many of them never reach our conscious mind. They surface for a millisecond and dissolve just as rapidly into the atmosphere, never to be experienced again. The ones that punch their way from a subconscious to a conscious state are the ones that stand a slight chance of being developed. Even then, the odds are not good. The trouble is that most of us don't realize that we're all walking/talking idea factories. We don't take the time to develop them and, more often than not, we're not even aware of them when they surface. Think of your mind as a large manufacturing plant capable of running around the clock nonstop. Unfortunately, the machinery is greased and ready, but it doesn't have the raw materials (ideas) to keep it going. As a result, hundreds of potentially good ideas are discarded, never to be analyzed, evaluated, or processed.

Merely saying that ideas are everywhere is not enough. The question is, How and where do we find them? Is snaring an idea like leaping into the air to catch a rising line drive? Unfortunately, no.

Each of us has to gather ideas in his own way. My system for idea gathering may seem ridiculous to you, just as your system may seem outright weird to me. A friend of mine who owns a discount specialty store routinely walks his dog at around midnight. Strange time to be out, but this is when he finds the peace and tranquility to think. "It's the best time of day," he says. "This is when I rest my mind and give it some much needed fresh air. It's also the time I get some of my best ideas. My defenses are down, I'm tired but relaxed, there are no schedules to meet, and I can go back and mull over thoughts and ideas that occurred to me during the day."

Others I spoke to find that ideas come easily to them when

biking, walking, reading, watching television, and through other forms of sport and entertainment. The best of the lot came from a travel agent who happens to be a fanatical video game freak. When he is not sending tourists to all parts of the world, he can be found in his den, which looks more like a Coney Island amusement arcade than it does a comfortable place to relax. The games blink, flash, bleep, and make all kinds of strange sounds.

"As soon as I get involved in a game, I forget about everything," he says. "It all slips into the foreground. It's almost like my mind shifts scenes. I'm on a different wavelength. While I'm all keyed up, I'm also relaxed. After an hour or so, I find that my mind has recharged itself and in the process good ideas come to me that can benefit me in my work and thus make my life easier."

A primary ingredient for successful idea recognition and development is relaxation. Everyone I spoke to stressed the fact that ideas flow most readily when one is relaxed. Relaxation can mean anything from cruising down the interstate with the radio blasting to listening to Respighi curled up on the sofa in your living room.

What about yourself? When do your best ideas come to you? During the day, at night, when playing or resting? Chances are they're most prevalent when your mind and body are in a resting state. As one psychologist put it, "The mind and body often have to be at half-speed in order for good ideas to surface."

But whether you're actively searching for ideas or just want to absorb everything you can in order to sift through masses of information for relevant tidbits, consider the following sources for ideas.

1. People (friends, relatives, acquaintances, strangers, business associates)
2. Conversations
3. Parties
4. Meetings
5. Exhibits, galleries
6. Museums
7. Flea markets
8. Films, concerts, theater, opera, ballet
9. Television
10. Store openings
11. Vacations

That's only a partial list. If we were to expand the above list, it would take up the greater part of this book. The point is that ideas are everywhere. Twenty-four hours a day, they're out there in the atmosphere waiting to be absorbed. It's squatters' rights. First come, first served. The first one to latch on to a potential idea, develop it, and make it work will reap the prize, bonus, raise, three-week special vacation, stock option, promotion, you name it. Kind of makes your mouth water when you think about it. I don't know about you, but the thought of latching on to that special idea or concept gets my adrenaline jolting through my body and I feel like running around the room at full throttle until I get it in the works.

Let's go further and consider other important factors for successful idea accumulation:

1. *Keep an open mind.* Don't make the mistake of prejudging an event, occasion, or meeting.

2. *Remember that great ideas are often discovered in unlikely places.* Often, the place where ideas are gathered has no bearing whatsoever on your work. Take another look at the above list. Ordinary conversations, for one, often trigger ideas. Sitting on a train going to work, you may pick up bits and pieces of three conversations going at once. None of them seem relevant, but if your antennae are up and consciously absorbing information from the atmosphere, all of a sudden, a word, phrase, sigh, gesture, argument, may trigger the germ of an idea. You never know. But if your system is shut down, you won't be able to sift through the millions of particles of conversation to find that speck of precious gold that may launch you and make you a front runner in your field. Inventors and scientists mentioned coming up with brilliant ideas at parties, while talking on the telephone, browsing through an art gallery, and even picking up necessities at a supermarket.

3. *Carry a notebook and pen with you at all times.* Then you can jot down ideas as they occur to you. Ideas often pass in waves and if they're not recorded immediately, they can be lost forever. So it's not worth letting ideas pass you by. You could be risking a lot. A million-dollar idea could have passed you in the night, and you were just too lazy to make a note on it.

Don't tempt fate and rely on memory. How many times have you said to yourself, *I'll remember, I'll remember,* and an hour later, you totally forget the thought. No, you're not absentminded. Forgetting is a human failing, especially if you lead a hectic life and you've got a lot on your mind. We're not computers. We can't depress buttons and recall ideas that are stored for safekeeping. Take no chances and record an idea as soon as it whips across your mind.

Once immersed in untold idea possibilities, let's go on and set idea goals.

CHAPTER 13
SET
IDEA
GOALS

We've surrounded ourselves with ideas. We know where they are, and how to latch on to them. Now what? Do we get our original ideas whenever we feel like it, when inspired, during a solar eclipse? None of the above.

Just as we set our sights on long-term career goals, let's be precise and set idea goals for ourselves. Are they not equally important? Career goals and idea goals have a great deal in common. A *career goal* involves a long-range plan where we work toward a specific position or goal, and an *idea goal* enhances and reinforces our chances of securing that long-term goal. They work together, each in its own separate way.

Be specific about your idea goals. Ideas are the heart, soul, and foundation of creativity. Without ideas, creativity could not take place. We cannot emphasize enough how important they are. They are priceless jewels that have to be protected and cherished.

An idea goal, like a career goal, is a commitment to yourself. More specifically, it's a promise to yourself to come up with a certain amount of ideas within a specified period of time on a given subject. For example, the ambitious secretary may set herself five idea goals per week—one to come up with an idea for improving her own efficiency, one to improve her boss's efficiency, and three more relating to improving general office efficiency. All of them, if realized, work to better and strengthen her position within her organization. The following week, however, she may set three idea goals or as many as ten idea goals and they may deal with something entirely different, such as ideas for new ways to increase the productivity of her company or possibly creating a new public relations campaign. The number and subject of your idea goals are unimportant; what matters is that you set yourself a creative challenge and then realize it.

Each of us develops his own system for setting idea goals. Some keep them in a separate notebook, others scribble them on whatever they happen to be reading at the time. An easy way to keep track of them is to jot them down on small index cards. I carry a little stack of them in my attaché case. When an idea pops into my head, I jot it down on a card, date it, put a subject heading on it, along with an approximate day for realizing it, and slip the card back in the stack.

It seems like a lot of work, but later on you'll appreciate the effort, because it will save you a great deal of time.

In the next few chapters, we'll talk about banking and gestating ideas. For now, let's try to keep them in a safe place.

The question is, How demanding should our idea goals be? Largely, it depends upon you and your work. If you're a super hustler, aggressive, the type of person who can't sit still for more than two minutes at a time, be tough on yourself and set weekly, even daily, idea goals. If you're tense, easily rattled, and have problems coping with stress, set idea goals that don't make you any more anxious than you already are. In other words, set idea goals you can live with and cope with. How much pressure and discomfort you place on yourself is relative. Generally speaking, I feel we can all benefit from moderate amounts of pressure. It keeps us on our toes, alert, and working toward our goals. By giving yourself an idea goal, you're giving yourself an assignment. Instead of a teacher, boss, supervisor, parent, or spouse telling you what has to be done and when it has to be done, you're giving it to yourself. You're making a contract with yourself. Break it, and you have to contend with yourself. In setting idea goals, keep the following factors in mind:

1. *Adjust idea goals to your work.* Since we all work at different jobs, it's nothing short of ridiculous to set common idea goals. Some of us are better off having daily goals, others weekly, and still others find monthly goals more compatible. A sales representative for a large jewelry manufacturer sets monthly goals. Since he's on the road practically eighty percent of the time, and the jewelry lines change seasonally, he finds that monthly idea goals make the most sense. He explains: "Since fashions, trends, and buying habits can change radically from season to season, to be effective and chalk up a good sales record, I have to come up with enticing gimmicks, sales approaches and strategies, discounts, suggestions, in order to entice customers to place big orders. That's the challenge for any creative salesperson in the jewelry business. To stay on my toes, I carry small index cards with me so I can jot down a good idea when it occurs to me. At the end of the month, I like to have at least ten ideas to rummage through in order to make some sensible decisions."

A senior electronics service technician specializing in building and repairing video games tries to come up with five good ideas a week. "If I don't come up with good ideas, I won't go anywhere in my work," he insists. "This is a highly competitive business. It's the people who come up with the great ideas who will go to the top. I don't intend to be a technician all my life. My goal is to design a new video game, manufacture it, market it, and clean up. Right now, I'm playing with blueprints for a prototype game. That's why I push myself to come up with five terrific ideas a week. Each time something occurs to me—a design, format, or marketing gimmick that I think may work—I write it down and number it. This way, when I'm ready to put it all together, I'll know exactly what I'm doing."

Many advertising copywriters and free-lance writers find that idea goals keep them motivated and working. One high-paid ad copywriter for a prestigious New York agency puts himself through the mill by giving himself a goal of two ideas a day. "Not just any ideas," he says. "I try to come up with ideas I know I can sell to my copy chief. And this obstacle is above and beyond my daily deadlines. It's kind of masochistic when I think about it, but I reason it's the only way I'm going to stay on top. After all, what is a copywriter without good ideas? He's useless, expendable, and he'll be booted from firm to firm. Why do you think there is so much turnover in this business. The bottom line is ideas. Without them, agencies wouldn't garner big accounts, and copywriters would be collecting unemployment insurance."

A free-lance magazine writer told me he tries to come up with at least five viable ideas a week. "If I don't come up with good article ideas, I'm out of business. Nothing very complicated about it. From time to time, magazine editors I've worked with over the years throw me a bone by giving me an assignment. It's terrific when it happens. But I can't depend upon it. I have to come up with ideas that sell, stories people want to read. My goal is five ideas and of that number I usually find that two or three are workable, or salable."

Regardless of what you do, make it a point to set idea goals. In the long run, you can't help profiting from it. As we said, you can be strict with yourself, but don't be so hard on yourself where meeting idea goals causes untold problems. That's a self-defeating strategy.

2. *Be flexible.* In this unpredictable work setting, situations can change radically from day to day. One day you're secure with a solid future ahead of you, the next your company has been reorganized, or taken over, and you find you're floating precariously in an uncertain sea. It happens all the time. What now? Reappraisal, new strategy, rethink idea goals.

No matter what happens, stay in control, and don't lose sight of your long-term career goals. As your situation changes, alter your idea goals accordingly. Whatever happens, keep all systems firing and you'll never be left in the wake.

Now that we have our ideas, what do we do with them?

CHAPTER 14
BANK YOUR
IDEAS

Things are looking up. We're sitting on some hot possibilities. But it seems like we've gone to a lot of trouble to set our ideas aside. Why all the fuss? Stay with me, and you'll see that there is a method to my madness. A dangerous mistake is making the immediate and sometimes rash determination regarding how good or bad an idea is and whether it's worth keeping.

Obviously, some ideas are better than others, a few are outright nonsense, and many more have only a microscopic particle of truth to them. Nevertheless, whether they be brilliant, great, good, mediocre, poor, or dumb, record them all. Let none get away.

Often our judgment is impaired by our mood. When you're in a terrific mood, every idea seems brilliant and when depressed, every idea seems miserable, silly, and not worth thinking about. Or if you're in one of those so-so "why bother" moods, somewhere between the devil and the deep blue sea, you'd just as soon not deal with anything. No matter how well you think you understand yourself, few people can be objective all the time. Our feelings, emotions, and moods get in our way. This is why it's important to bank ideas until you're ready to view them objectively. You'll be surprised at what you'll find. That silly idea may seem brilliant in the sunlight, or conversely, what you thought was a brilliant idea may seem like embarrassing drivel.

Consider the following suggestions:

1. *File ideas by date or category.* The system you choose is up to you; use whichever makes more sense. If you're involved in many different projects, it may be better to file ideas by category. Take the ad copywriter who's handling five different accounts, each of which is very different from the next. In this case, why not set up files for each account so ideas can be filed in the appropriate place? If all your work centers around one topic— electronics, food handling, microelectronics, pocket computers—one idea file will do the trick.

2. *Do a preliminary evaluation.* Before filing, note impressions, thoughts, and observations. They can be valuable when you view your ideas later on. These off-the-cuff impressions may help you make further determinations and lead to still further insights. Also, when relevant, note place, conditions, and circumstances under which an idea is recorded. You may find this information valuable as well.

3. *Keep your idea file in a convenient place.* Don't be scattered. Knowing how important order is, make sure your idea file is accessible when you need it.

4. *Keep ideas short and to the point.* This way, when you go back to them, they're easy to read and digest. Try not to be wordy. Think in short, clear, tight, telegraph-like sentences. It makes for an easy undertanding and further interpretation and elaboration.

Once ideas are banked, now what? Do we leave them for our grandchildren, or go back to them the next day? Give up? Neither one. The answer is, Let them gestate. Webster's definition of *gestate* is "to conceive and gradually develop in the mind." An easy way to understand gestation is to think of the process of aging wines. What happens when you age wine? If you do what a knowledgeable wine merchant tells you to do, you put a bottle (or bottles) of wine aside for a number of weeks, months, even years. While the wine is sitting undisturbed, a chemical process, popularly known as aging, takes place, which sharpens, softens, or enhances the taste of the wine. In short, at the end of the aging process, your wine not only tastes better than it would have tasted if you drank it immediately, it has also appreciated in price. Now you know why wine freaks buy cases of wine cheap, and stow it away in their cellars for a period of time. It's a smart move when you consider what you're getting in return.

Now let's apply the same aging principles to our ideas. Instead of aging our ideas, we're letting them gestate. By banking our ideas, we're allowing a much needed gestation period. You'll soon see that distance provides all kinds of unforeseen rewards. A little time can turn a superficial, subjective reading into an intelligent objective reading. It never fails: walk away from a situation, come back thirty minutes later, and chances are you'll see it in a new light.

Early in my career, I was taught the benefits of letting copy gestate for a while. When working for newspapers, time was a luxury I seldom had. Nevertheless, I learned to make do. Even when faced with daily deadlines, I tried to put a story aside for an hour and then go back and edit and rewrite it if need be. It never failed. That one-hour gestation period, brief as it was, provided enough distance to help me make major improvements in the story and pick up glaring inconsistencies I missed when writing my first draft.

When I had time, I lengthened the gestation period to a day and, when possible, a weekend. I find that a couple of days are ideal for heightening judgment and fine-tuning critical abilities.

Apply the same principles to the ideas you've banked. How much time should you allow? Remember the following:

- It's foolish to try and recommend an all-purpose gestation period that's right for everyone. Some of us need a few days, others a week, and still others find that a month-long separation from their ideas does wonders for honing their objective powers. It's up to you.
- Whatever time period you decide upon, be consistent in your patterns.

• Word of caution. Letting too much time pass is not a good idea either since you risk losing interest and excitement.

At the end of the gestation period, you'll be delighted to see things in a new light. The good ideas will be strengthened, fleshed out, and taken through their various stages, ready to go. The poor ideas will be permanently filed in the wastepaper basket, never to be seen again. The weak ones may go back into your gestation file for another week until you're ready to make a decision.

CHAPTER 15
BRAINSTORM

Let's jump ahead a bit. You've got the idea of ideas. You've banked it, let it gestate, it feels right, and all your instincts tell you it's a surefire winner. However, you're stumped. The idea is just sitting in your brain unable to move. Momentary mental paralysis. You weren't expecting this. Now what? Your mind was running at full speed, now you just don't know how to proceed.

It's not uncommon. It often happens when you're under the gun and facing a major deadline, or when the boss is breathing down your neck waiting for ideas so he can mollify the brass above him. The more pressure that's applied by yourself and others, the more blocked you become.

One solution is *brainstorming*. What is brainstorming? Simply, it is an approach to problem solving. It can also be used for searching for and expanding upon ideas. The nice part about brainstorming is that you need nothing more elaborate than a few sharpened pencils, a couple of legal pads, and an active imagination (or imaginations).

There are two types of brainstorming: brainstorming alone and brainstorming with others. Depending upon your personality, adopt the method that best suits you. Most people prefer the latter method, since it requires less imagination and creative input.

Brainstorming with Others

Using the group method, you can form a homogeneous or a heterogeneous group. Let's look at each one.

Homogeneous group. Whatever the problem, idea, or concept you wish to explore, form a group of people who have a background or expertise in the subject. For instance, you head your own paper company and your goal is to market a new type of paper, and you want input regarding the most effective way to get it to the public and stimulate interest. Your group may consist of knowledgeable people from your own company, notably paper salespeople, in-house manufacturing experts, and advertising and public relations people. Every member of the group is well versed in the paper industry.

Heterogeneous group. Instead of forming a group made up of experts in the paper industry to solve our paper problem, we're going to find people with different backgrounds who we think will help us come up with first-rate ideas. We'll call upon a toy distributor, a high-ranking packaging expert, a management consultant, a couple of recent MBA graduates, and the president of an office supply house.

The above grouping only sounds bizarre. In practice, the results can be surprising. The trick is gathering the right mixture of people. Don't take the word *heterogeneous* too literally. In putting together your group, keep the following pointers in mind:

1. *Make sure group members possess problem-solving abilities.* Look at the assemblage of experts gathered to solve our paper

marketing problem. None of them work in the paper industry, yet each one possesses advanced business expertise. The reason for forming a heterogeneous group is that it is desirable to bring fresh blood to a problem. By bringing together people who work in different industries, you're providing a new perspective, a fresh slant to the problem.

2. *Just anyone won't do.* Don't go too far in your attempt to find fresh blood. Remember, there has to be a basis, an underlying logic for putting the group together. If it's a major business problem that needs solving, I wouldn't put together a group consisting of three machinists, two tool and die makers, and four air traffic controllers. A group like this might be suitable for a complex technical problem that taps each member's technical/mechanical expertise, but it doesn't have the business acumen to solve a problem that has a number of high-ranking executives baffled.

Which method should I choose? If you're waiting for me to tell you which method is best, I'm sorry, I don't have the answer. It depends upon the problem. If you have the time, it doesn't hurt to experiment with both methods. As a rule of thumb, though, complex, highly technical problems require a fairly homogeneous grouping of people with similar expertise. However, you have more latitude with problems of a general nature. Here you can experiment with different groupings of people. If it's a general business problem, for example, you can form a group consisting of people from twelve different businesses and come to a speedy and successful resolution to a problem. Again, planning, logic, and an understanding of human nature are needed to put together any group, be it a homogeneous or a heterogeneous group.

Brainstorming technique. Whether you have a homogeneous or a heterogeneous group, the brainstorming method follows similar patterns. With a pencil and legal pad in front of each member, structure the meeting as follows:

1. *Appoint a group leader to control the session.* To avoid chaos, and ten or fifteen people shouting opinions at the same time, a brainstorming session needs a leader. Often the leader is the person who forms the group or, if it's a group formed by a high-ranking executive of a company, that person will most probably run the session. Whatever conditions prompted the session, make sure a capable, dominant, outspoken person is leading the group. This person must be aggressive enough to make himself

heard, and he must be able to control the movement of the group.

2. *Appoint a secretary.* This is a vital job. This person is going to record the blood and guts of the meeting by taking notes at supersonic speed. Afterward, the notes will be typed and edited and the finished product will be presented to the various members. The secretary has to have her eyes and ears open. Not only must she know and understand what is said, but who said it as well. This is important information, and not only for the problem at hand; when the session is over, it's good to know who contributed the most valuable input. When putting together other brainstorming sessions, you'll want to gather those insightful people who can get things done quickly and efficiently, and who know how to reason in group settings.

3. *Identify the goals and aims of the meeting.* With a leader and a secretary appointed, we're ready to begin. The leader identifies the goals of the meeting. If there are multigoals, an order of priorities is established. From the outset, the meeting is going to proceed logically and with a system. For complex problems, subgoals or subproblems often have to be identified and resolved. Let's say the major problem of the brainstorming session is reducing estimated costs on a new construction project by twenty-five percent in order to work within a tight budget. Once this is resolved, the group can move on to the subgoal, which is laying a foundation in two months as opposed to three months. Now the group faces the challenge of finding ways to cut corners, adopt new work strategies, and find cost-effective ways of utilizing labor.

4. *Encourage each person to express opinions.* Until everyone warms up and ideas are batted about freely, move in a circular fashion, allowing each person to render an opinion. When all opinions are expressed, the conversation can proceed effortlessly, moving to anyone who has something to say.

5. *Stay with one problem (or issue) until it is resolved.* This makes for clarity. Don't let your discussions get out of hand by allowing several topics to be discussed at once.

6. *When there is disagreement, search for clarity, meaning, common ground, and objectivity.* Remember why you're there. It's to solve a problem, not to get your own way.

7. *Avoid emotional outpourings.* Keep emotions out of brainstorming sessions. It's all right to argue a point vehemently, but remember that objectivity is the goal. This means discussion aimed at gathering facts, so conclusions can be drawn.

8. *Try voting.* If opinions can't be clarified and refined, try coming to a common ground by voting. This is a last resort. If you're at the end of a long brainstorming session and you've gotten nowhere, before ending the session *in medias res*, vote on a course of action or topic to be discussed when the session is resumed. Often, it takes several sessions to arrive at a satisfactory conclusion.

9. *Clarify and refine the major points.* At the conclusion of a successful brainstorming session, make sure that points and conclusions are crystal clear and that there is agreement on the proposed course of action. Don't conclude if there are rough edges yet to be smoothed out. Let each person have a final say.

Brainstorming Alone

Group brainstorming is quite common within business organizations. But what if you don't work in a group setting? You're a one-person business who also faces major problems. You're an architect, attorney, accountant, systems analyst, interior decorator, industrial designer, fashion designer, cartoonist, copywriter, jewelry maker, potter, writer, painter, and so on. What do you do when faced with what appears to be an unsolvable problem, an idea that won't take shape? You can shelve it temporarily, forget about it, or solve it by brainstorming. If you choose brainstorming, you'll use a somewhat different method than the one described above. Instead of putting together a homogeneous or heterogeneous group, you'll use your imagination and concoct one yourself, and create the input that each member normally provides.

An architect acquaintance says he uses this method all the time. From time to time he faces a problem he can't solve. Instead of forging ahead on gut feeling, he creates a scenario of characters who pose questions and objections to the project at hand. Questions are raised by imaginary critics from different quarters—builders, designers, accountants, manufacturers. Each poses problems and obstacles that the architect must hurdle before his problem can be solved. He goes as far as engaging in imaginary conversations with his critics so he can expand his ideas and present his arguments in detail. Objectivity and honesty are called for. Based upon past experience, knowledge of the field, and anticipated criticism, you have to create a cast of characters you'll encounter in the real world.

Not everyone can pull this off. Beyond imagination, it takes a good deal of confidence to bat arguments around by yourself. You're like a ventriloquist assuming many different roles at will.

Let's try brainstorming alone.

1. *Set the stage.* Since you're a one-person organization, you're going to set the stage, and carefully pick the people you need to carry off the session. Instead of gathering live bodies, you're going to put together a group of imaginary characters who will give you a clear idea how to develop your idea and probe problems and obstacles you can expect along the way. Picking the right imaginary characters who will objectively screen or develop your idea is no easy chore. Pick people who will both support and criticize your work so you'll get an unbiased, realistic picture. Think of the architect in the example cited. In his imaginary group he assembled builders, designers, accountants, manufacturers—all the key people who will present an accurate perspective of his work.

2. *Create round table discussion.* There is just so much you can keep in your head. Now that you have five or six, or possibly more, people in your imaginary group, with pencil in hand, place them around a table. You're doing pretty much the same thing you'd do in setting up a live brainstorming session, except that the characters are in your head. Once you know where everyone is, begin.

3. *Establish the problem clearly.* What is it you want to accomplish, prove, develop, solve? Just as you'd brainstorm in a group, the problem has to be crystal clear. A good way to fine-tune your problem is to write it down, stare at it, and then sharpen it, if you have to.

4. *Begin the discussion.* Loosen up because this is where the fun begins. Make sure you're in a comfortable place where you'll feel free to talk and expand upon ideas all by yourself. Let's be honest, if the wrong people happen to hear you, they'll question your sanity. Can you blame them? Close the doors, and find a quiet place so you can let your hair down and talk, shout, and get to the guts of your problem quickly. Just as you stated your problem clearly, keep a record of each person's opposing or supportive views. As you move from one imaginary person to the next, make sure the different comments are clearly stated on paper. Since you're all alone, it's easy to become stuck in one place and lose

track of the discussion. As you become involved in probing all aspects and angles of your problem, jot down your observations and comments from your imaginary cast of experts.

5. *Break the whole into parts.* To make problem solving easier, you may find it easier to break your idea (or germ of an idea) into its component parts. The more parts you create, the more effective and thorough the approach, the easier it is to understand and expand. One workable approach is carving your idea into ten parts. Once completed, try to break those ten parts into still smaller subdivisions. By so doing, you're giving your idea greater depth.

6. *Free associate.* If the above approach isn't compatible and you're in a rut and can't go any further, try free associating. Whether brainstorming alone or in a group, free associating is a great way to come up with a whole slew of ideas and thoughts quickly. Pencil in hand, focus on the problem and write down anything that comes to mind. Initially, it doesn't matter whether the thoughts are directly related to the problem. The reason for free association is to get the mind warmed up and cooking. Free associating can be compared to having someone give your car a push when you can't get it started. Once your creative machinery is revved up, you slowly build momentum. Thoughts that were random and unfocused become tight and focused, and you rapidly begin to hone in on the problem. If starting is difficult, try closing your eyes, relax, and let your mind take off in a million and one different directions. Be patient; before you know it, ideas and random thoughts will begin to collide in front of you.

Keep in mind that breaking a whole into several parts and free association are only suggestions for helping you brainstorm alone. There is no tried-and-true pattern for getting results. Since this is essentially a free-form technique, find the most comfortable path that leads to results and stick to it.

7. *Summarize and finalize the results.* If you're able to make some interesting breakthroughs by brainstorming alone, don't quit until you're satisfied with your results and it's all down on paper. Often, last-minute insights, thoughts, and observations are lost. Make sure nothing gets by you and everything is crystal clear. If your session with yourself is successful, you've established a plan or course of action, you've gained insight, learned something. You started with nothing and, within a couple of hours, you've managed to direct yourself toward your goal.

By the same token, if you're unable to make progress, stimulate your imagination, relax, and uninhibitedly create a scenario of characters, abandon the project. It's not the end of the world. As I said, not everyone can brainstorm alone. Some of us are comfortable enough to pull it off, others cannot. If you can't do it, try brainstorming in a group. In other words, find the method that works best for *you*.

Whether you brainstorm alone or in a group (homogeneous or heterogeneous), you can't help but profit from the experience in some way. Even if it doesn't provide immediate answers to your problems, it can't help setting the stage for making clear, precise, well-thought-out decisions.

Once your idea is thoroughly brainstormed and you're ready to take it to the next step, prepare yourself for opposition and criticism. To contend with it, you'll have to create an impenetrable wall of excitement and enthusiasm around yourself. Let's find out more.

CHAPTER 16 GENERATE EXCITEMENT FOR YOUR IDEA

As we said in Part One, Chapter Five, "Overcoming Barriers to Creativity," you must be prepared to cope with barriers in your path. You may be sitting on the greatest invention since the wheel but the people you have to convince and sell may be indifferent (even hostile) to it at first. The difficult part is not letting other people's indifference, pessimism, or negativity discourage you. No matter who you are or where you're working, it's unreasonable to expect excitement and support from all sectors. When it's missing, you have to generate it yourself. This requires a huge and sometimes exhausting energy investment. It means mentally preparing yourself for all contingencies. The challenge is turning a negative response into a positive one. Look upon it as a battle of wits.

Imagine you're holding the widget of widgets, the one that will make people's lives easier. How can I get people excited? How do I transfer my excitement to others?

No matter what you're trying to accomplish, it involves finding your own way and devising systems and approaches that fire others' imaginations. An executive in charge of the research and development division of a national cereal company told me that every time he makes a new product presentation, he mentally prepares himself beforehand. Along with a carefully planned presentation, he repeats the following affirmations to himself several times before he walks into the meeting: "I will not be defeated," and "I will convince and excite others."

It's a practical approach, one that never fails to deliver positive results. By almost chanting the two affirmations to himself over and over again, he preprograms himself for success. His mind is clear and his mission is more than obvious. Relying on intense concentration and unquestioning belief in his work, he won't settle for anything but *acceptance*.

An enterprising accountant told me he relishes competition because it makes him stronger and helps build a solid defense against criticism. "To do my best, I like to be excited and charged about my work, especially when I'm making a pitch for a new account," he says. "I overcome anything in my way by playing a little game with myself. I go in to a new situation expecting opposition and criticism. Consequently, I'm prepared to deal with it. I look upon the whole thing as a great big game. It's simple that way. The object of a game is to *win*. But in order to make that game fun and exciting, and that victory all the more pleasurable, you have to be prepared to sweat, work, and do some hustling. This way when you win, you can *taste* your victory, and feel good all over. When I walk into a fiercely competitive situation with this attitude, it's almost impossible to knock me down. I've worked on myself to the point where I won't accept anything but conquest. I'm like a fighter who psyches himself up before going into the ring."

Like the accountant in the above example, you have to come across like a tornado of excitement and determination. To help build that indestructible wall of enthusiasm, consider the following suggestions:

1. *Devise an approach that will fire the imaginations of other people.* Just coming up with a good idea is not enough. Knowing the needs of the marketplace, and the demands of your su-

periors, what kind of an approach and format can you put together that will knock everyone clear out of their seats? Examine it from every angle until you come up with something totally new and revolutionary; something that will convince friends *and foes* in record-breaking time.

2. *Fantasize success.* Start off on the right foot by fantasizing success and the results you hope to achieve. Before you make that difficult presentation or sales pitch, or before you propose an expensive project that will double earnings next year, see and imagine the finish line. That's where you'll be when you accomplish what you set out to do. By walking into a tough situation fantasizing success and victory, you're already buoyed up for all eventualities.

3. *Surround yourself with allies.* In order to build that solid wall of excitement, you'll need help. Whether it's one, three, or fifty, attract others who will support you and fight for your idea. Don't think of yourself as the Lone Ranger, a lonely creative bastion fighting towering forces who hope to maintain the status quo. In any organization, there's bound to be at least one other individual who thinks and feels the way you do. Find that person (or persons) and form a liaison so you can both rally against the opposition and achieve your goals. No matter how brilliant your idea, in order to make it work, you'll need a solid support network to convince others.

4. *Benefit from competition.* Competition is healthy. It channels and focuses your creativity. It keeps you on your toes—alert, aware, and ready to deal with those who threaten your terrain. Instead of looking upon it as a threat, which is the normal negative reaction, think of it as a challenge and a rallying point for showing what you can do. Who will make it over the finish line first?

To function at peak creative efficiency, you must get to a point where you can generate your own excitement and not be sidetracked by those who attempt to discourage you from making headway. Always be prepared to meet pessimisim with optimism and confidence. Most important, never lose sight of your goal, for that will keep you excited, motivated, and working at fever pitch throughout every stage of the creative process.

CHAPTER 17
GIVE
YOURSELF
A BREAK!

"All work and no play makes Jack a dull boy." There's an awful lot of truth to that old adage.

In a high-powered success-oriented society like ours, it's very easy to become a workaholic. Most of us are brought up staunchly believing in the virtues of the Puritan Work Ethic. The harder we work, the more we'll get back. To a certain extent, this is true. Carried too far, it borders on a dangerous compulsion.

The scenario is all too familiar. The more successful we become, the more we fear taking time off to rest and enjoy ourselves. The overriding fear is that if we allow ourselves too much free time we'll miss out on something, or possibly someone will take our place, usurp our territory. As a result, we're always on guard, seven days a week, 365 days a year. Two-week vacations and even long weekends are greeted with mixed feelings. To stay on top of things, we take our attaché cases away with us and religiously call our offices once a day, rain or shine.

The above description may be somewhat extreme, yet millions of us, whether we admit it to ourselves or not, display many of the workaholic's symptoms. In working toward success, and maximum creativity, we neglect other important needs. As one New York psychologist put it, "It's very easy to get caught up in our own success struggles. In working toward long-term success goals, we become neurotically disciplined about our work and undisciplined about other areas of our lives. As often happens, we wind up neglecting our basic need for rest. It's analogous to not giving our bodies enough food. The dramatic difference is we're consciously aware of our need for food, and often unconsciously aware of our need for rest."

Deprive our system of adequate rest and, not only will it stop being creative, it will break down. There is nothing very mysterious about it. What are we but biological machines? Just as a machine needs fuel, lubricants, maintenance, the human machine similarly needs food, rest, and periodic maintenance to function well.

If we dangerously abuse ourselves, we face the debilitating contemporary malady popularly known as "burn-out." Coined by Dr. Herbert J. Freudenberger, the term describes the breakdown of our systems and a loss of interest in the world around us. All of a sudden and for no apparent reason, our well-oiled and seemingly high-functioning machines begin to misfire. Our work performance is affected; our personal lives are thrown into a tailspin; where we were once rooted to a life style, we now feel fragmented; enthusiasm is replaced by disenchantment; high energy involvement gives way to apathetic disinterest; creativity diminishes markedly.

All of the above spell burn-out. Dr. Freudenberger blames the times in which we live, taking in all the crucial elements of our lives, from technology, new attitudes and behavior patterns, and drastically changing social customs (high divorce figures), to redefined ethics and morals (the sexual revolution). "We are living in times of change so rapid they've left us without moorings," he says in his book, *Burn-Out*.

Who's prone to burn-out? High-functioning, hard-working, aggressive people. In short, most of us.

What are the symptoms? Freudenberger lists a number of

symptoms, among which are lack of enthusiasm, overwork, disenchantment, forgetfulness, irritability, physical complaints (headaches, pains), disorientation, diminished sex drive, and so on.

As long as we're experiencing the debilitating effects of burnout, our creativity is stalled, just as the rest of our being ceases to function at maximum efficiency.

How do we combat it? There are a number of things that can be done; most important is getting in touch with ourselves so that we are aware of what is happening. As one victim of burn-out put it: "It took me almost six months to realize that everything was getting out of hand. I couldn't put my finger on the causes. It's not like my job or marriage was threatened. Both were secure. The feelings that most confused me were a lack of incentive and drive. Where I once bounded through the day, I now crawled through it without enthusiasm. I became so depressed and withdrawn, I went into therapy and over a three-month period, I began to see what was happening. I needed time to be alone to think and to put things in perspective. Things were going so fast, I could no longer keep up. As a result, my system rebelled and almost stopped functioning."

This man was so uncomfortable that he sought professional help. Not everyone who experiences burn-out seeks professional help. However, it's important to point out that most people who suffer from it experience feelings of isolation, and even alienation. And it often takes a period of painful soul searching to get to the root of the problem.

When the symptoms of burn-out surface, the first thing we have to do is apply the brakes and slow down all our systems— physical and mental. Once done, we have to look at our lives from a qualitative perspective. Just as a cold and sore throat are signals from our body telling us to slow down and repair ourselves, the symptoms of burn-out are warnings that things have gotten out of control, that it's time to reappraise our lives, and find and patch the troublespots.

Dr. Freudenberger frequently mentions the necessity of being alone with ourselves in order to fully experience what he calls "aloneness." "We run from ourselves every chance we get," he says. "Think about it. When did you last spend time by yourself, with yourself, doing something you enjoy? With yourself is the important thing to check, because much of the time we're alone we shut off our minds and feelings. We get involved in a television program or have a couple of drinks or fall asleep. We're not really there for ourselves in a related kind of way. We're merely alone. Being alone *with* yourself, however, means your senses are alive, your thoughts are keeping you company, you're sitting in that room or going to that art gallery with a person, not just an empty body. You're sharing an experience *with* yourself, and you're enjoying it."

Advice worth considering. Aside from getting in touch with yourself, it's also important to talk about and delve into your feelings with someone you trust, be it a spouse, friend, or relative. In a society that rewards and idolizes the rugged individualists among us, we are obsessed with going it alone. Reaching out to others for help is often construed as weakness, a sign that we're not able to handle things. But if our goal is to operate at maximum efficiency, and be as creative as our abilities and intellects allow, all channels must be open, so information can flow in and out without obstructions in the way.

Ironically, many of us have to learn to rest. As infants, no one had to teach us how to rest. It was something we did naturally any time of the day or night. As we get older and our need for rest diminishes, we carelessly abuse and push ourselves beyond our limits. We scorn sleep and even simple rest as an intrusion and sometimes as a weakness of mind and body. And so we do with less sleep, five or six hours a night instead of seven or eight. Our workday often begins before nine and goes straight through until seven, or after, with only a midday break for lunch, which often amounts to a low-keyed but nevertheless pressured business engagement.

With schedules crammed full of activity from morning till night, we fail to see that there are many opportunities to pause for rest. Using the suggestions outlined below, you'll see that it is not as difficult as you thought. All it takes is ingenuity and planning.

1. *Find time to be alone.* Not just during the workweek, but on weekends as well. Often, our weekends can be as hectic as our workdays. Make it a point to find a convenient time when you're not overburdened with people demanding your attention. This is going to be your special time when you can do something that pleases you, when you're going to shut down all systems and close all valves and switches, so information is neither coming in nor going out.

Many busy people mentioned midafternoon as an ideal time

for rest. At this point we begin to slow down; our minds and bodies are calling for rest. It's also the time when we tend to push ourselves by pouring coffee into our systems to temporarily recharge ourselves so we can make it through the rest of the day.

2. *Use even brief periods of time for rest.* We're not suggesting you turn your desk light off, drop everything, walk out, and return an hour later. Few of us can do that without facing serious repercussions. But we can stop for a brief amount of time to collect ourselves and just rest. The amount of time is not important. Some of us can stop for a half hour, others can spare only fifteen minutes. It's not the quantity, but the *quality*, of time that's important. Each person's recuperative powers are different. There are people who have trained themselves to meditate for a mere ten minutes and report feeling recharged and renewed.

3. *Plan vacations.* Vacations are important. Most of us take them, but only a small minority use them to good advantage. As we said in the opening paragraphs of this section, millions of people go off on their annual two-week vacation tense, anxiety-ridden, unable to sever ties with their work.

Needless to say, it's almost impossible to rest, relax, and rebuild your worn-out system if you're uptight about a fellow worker usurping your terrain. To avoid this, try taking a number of short vacations throughout the year. If two weeks away from the office makes you uneasy, why not take a week at a time? That way you won't feel as if you're totally out of control. Throughout the year, try getting away for a few long weekends. Pack spouse and family up, get in the car, and head into the country. A change in scenery can do wonders.

For these short jaunts, do yourself a favor and leave your attaché case home. While you're at it, leave your wrist watch home also. Instead, take a couple of novels, mysteries, or biographies. For two days, slip into a relaxed, easygoing time frame. Within no time, you'll feel like a new person. In the process of unwinding, you may be pleasantly surprised when a number of winning ideas come to you out of nowhere. If you forgot, in Chapter Twelve, we mentioned vacations as a suggested resource for ideas. No matter how you look at it, vacations are not only necessary, they also serve to enhance your creativity.

4. *Define rest in your own terms.* What should you do during rest periods? Anything that gives you pleasure and takes your mind off everything. A speech therapist we spoke to finds a quiet

place and meditates for fifteen minutes; a pharmacist engages in a heated game of chess with himself for close to half an hour; and a real estate agent walks around the block for ten minutes.

Each person in resting in his own way. Think about this and answer these questions: What is the ideal time to stop and rest? What can I do during that period to give me a sense of peace and renewal?

CHAPTER 18
GET PHYSICAL!

Technology has its good and bad points. While it has stream-lined our lives and made everything a lot easier, at work and home, it's also made us lazy. Without being aware of it, millions of us have sunk into a cushiony, sedentary life style where we practically pivot from one sitting position to another.

Beyond rest, we need periods of exercise in order to connect our minds and bodies, and find our mind/body connection. The R&R breaks outlined in the previous chapter are primarily de-signed to turn off our minds. But within a hectic week we also have to set aside a time for exercise, for an activity that provides an outlet, or for an escape valve from the anxieties and pressures of our fast-paced lives. Ask anybody who exercises religiously and they'll tell you about the freedom and pleasure they get from a heated workout. They'll describe feelings of elation, escape, and boundless energy. What's more, it reroutes and changes the energy flow, allowing them to be more creative in their work. Exercise acts as both a psychological and physical tune-up. The results are a fresh outlook and greater creativity.

There's a reason why millions of Americans jog every day. Avid joggers will tell you that it's both physically and mentally gratifying. An ultrasound technician working in a large urban hospital runs between six and eight miles a day. He describes the sensation of running: "It's not always easy crawling out of bed when it's still dark to run. Often I feel like forgetting about it, and crawling under the covers to get another hour of sleep. But I force myself to do it and I never regret it. The first ten minutes of running are the hardest. After that, I begin to feel great. The more I run, the more energized I become. I never push myself and I maintain a pace that's comfortable for me. The best part is when I develop a steady motion, I begin to relax and all my defenses melt away. I'm in my own secure little world. I'm aware of other joggers passing me, yet I'm turned off to them. For the better part of my run, I'm in my own space, free from bills, pressures and people. As far as I'm concerned, it's the only way to find peace of mind."

Mike Spino, author of *Mike Spino's Mind/Body Running Program*, says running can trigger an altered, or heightened, state of consciousness. While running, you slip into another world, and in the process new energy, insights, and thought processes are triggered. The repetitive motion of running is compared to the experience achieved through meditation. Writes Spino: "Running has provided me with some of the most intense and memorable inner experiences I have ever known—experiences unlike any others I've ever had, experiences so unique they don't lend themselves to conventional description."

You don't have to be a runner to experience similar feelings. You can achieve the same results engaging in any number of physical activities. Other people I've spoken to described similar sensations from biking, roller skating, calisthenic routines, and playing racquetball.

A free-lance systems analyst who works out of his converted barn high in the Vermont hills takes a forty-five-minute-to-an-hour break every day to chop wood. Like jogging, handball, or biking, he becomes immersed in the motion of his activity and the pressures of the world slip into the far periphery. A 45-year-old Chicago-based criminal lawyer boxes three times a week for an hour at a stretch. The workout is exhausting, yet he reports feeling refreshed and rejuvenated after each one.

Whatever physical activity you engage in, remember the following:

1. *You're not out to become a champion jogger, skater, or boxer.* To achieve maximum benefit, have no expectations or goals. It's the quality, not the quantity, of the workout that counts. It doesn't matter whether you bike or jog five or twenty-five miles a day. If you feel better after a workout, you've accomplished what you set out to do. Soon enough your attitude, creativity, and productivity will improve. You'll feel charged, renewed, energized, and, as often happens, new ideas, concepts, and thoughts will surface.

2. *Find a comfortable time to exercise.* Ideal times to jog, walk, bike, or do calisthenics are early morning or early evening. They're quiet, serene times of the day when no one is breathing down your neck.

3. *Find a compatible pace and stick to it.* Some people prefer to bike or jog with others. Yet, to experience inner peace and calm, and recharge your creative machinery, I suggest exercising alone—in the beginning, at any rate. It may take time, but once you establish a comfortable and relaxed pace, you'll enjoy exploring the hidden spaces in your mind you never knew existed. In the process, you'll learn more about yourself and discover new sources of creative energy.

4. *Exercise frequently.* You don't have to exercise seven days a week. However, once a week accomplishes little. To free mind and body and enjoy maximum benefits from your workout, I suggest nothing less than three or four times a week.

You say you hate physical exercise? If I can't convert you, let me offer an alternate suggestion. Have you tried *games?* They're not physical, but they can sharpen and refresh your creative powers. I was surprised to learn that many creative people indulge in games. The most obvious reason is enjoyment, but the reason I found most intriguing was that they strengthened their creative powers.

What kind of games? You name it. Anything from chess, Parcheesi, Scrabble, Boggle, Monopoly, bridge, or poker to checkers.

A senior vice president of a solar equipment company told me he's passionate about Monopoly. At least once a week, he, wife, and teenage son sit down for a long and sometimes heated game of Monopoly. "Ever since I was a kid, I enjoyed playing Monopoly," he says. "The only difference is when I was younger, it was just a fantasy game. Now, however, I find that I often connect the game to my business life. The great part about the game is I can take reckless chances I'd never take in real life. Inevitably, I adopt strategies I employ in my work. What happens is the creative juices start moving. While negotiating a high-priced property and control over one part of the board, I say to myself, *What do I have to do to expedite these moves so I give up little in return?* It's a question I routinely ask myself at work."

Games serve multiple purposes. They provide relaxation and diversion, yet they also require intelligence, cunning, and, yes, creative input. To master any of the popular games, tact and strategy are required. Like real life, the goal is to win and reap a reward.

A mechanical engineer with a major construction company plays chess every chance he gets. On a quiet Sunday at home, logs crackle in the fireplace and Beethoven pours from two stereo speakers while he's immersed in a tense game of chess with a neighbor. Why *chess?* "It fires my imagination, stimulates me, and helps me solve problems," he explains. "The great part about chess is no one is pressuring me into moving. I can take my time and ponder each move. In the process of deciding what I'm going to do, I find that energy channeled into the game is unconsciously diverted to problems I face at work. Without realizing it, my mind is focused on two different levels, each of which is working independently. I can't tell you how many times I unravel difficult work-related problems while hunched over a chessboard."

Maybe you've achieved similar results playing a game you enjoy. Sometimes we have to shut down part of our machines in order for other parts to take over and work on their own steam. While immersed in a game, our relaxed, tension-free minds often wander to problems that plague us.

Imagine being faced with a difficult problem and, no matter how hard you try, the solution evades you. Of course, you can take the problem home with you and sit up to all hours of the night trying to find the answer. But chances are you won't get very far. If you're at an impassable barrier, the best thing to do is stop, regroup, divert your energy.

Forget about the problem and immerse yourself in a game you enjoy. Allow mind and body to cool down. The game of Scrabble, for instance, seems to have this effect on a lot of people. Since it requires so much concentration, all your energy is focused on formulating clever words with which to outsmart your opponents. Don't think for a moment that the problem that troubles you has disappeared. It's only lingering in your subconscious waiting for more information and direction. In the midst of a game, you may be pleasantly surprised when your mind takes a brief but enlightening voyage to the problem you've been batting around for days, offering the solution you've been waiting for.

A financial planner with an international conglomerate finds that an infrequent game of Scrabble during a lunch break helps him solve problems. However, this executive prefers to play the game alone since it gives him the opportunity to use all his powers of concentration.

So whether it's games or exercise, I urge you to try one or both. Aside from providing a sense of renewal, they're ideal for focusing, channeling and stimulating your creative energy.

CHAPTER 19
KEEP YOUR
CREATIVE
VALVES OPEN

Ideally, the need and urge to extend your creativity should carry over to all aspects of your life. To function fully and make the most of your life, keep your creative channels open twenty-four hours a day. Many of us shut the creative spigot as soon as the workday ends. Instead of closing it, leave it open just enough so ideas and concepts are still sifted and analyzed. By allowing your system to run at half speed, your creative powers will work all by themselves in unconscious or subconscious seclusion.

Few of us can function at full throttle fourteen hours a day. To maintain maximum efficiency and work at our creative peaks, it's important that we vary our paces, and adjust the flow of creative energy to our body's physiological and psychological rhythms.

Living creatively means allowing *everything* to touch you. To enjoy maximum creativity, try to make every minute experience count. Let nothing pass you by. Take a holistic, rather than a mechanistic or circumscribed, view of your life and work in relation to the world around you. According to the *mechanistic* view, things happen separately and by themselves, whereas a *holistic* view implies that all things are interrelated. In sum, a unity, or oneness, infuses our lives.

Instead of seeing your life as compartmentalized and broken down into separate functions, take the broader view and look for meaning within the larger scheme of things. As opposed to reducing everything to function and category, see responsibilities, chores, tasks, and time periods as *related* parts of an integrated life plan. Like the ancient Taoist view of life, fashion a philosophy that views the universe as a unified entity. This automatically puts everything you do in a related perspective. It roots your life to deeper meanings, and encourages creativity on many fronts.

To accomplish this, consider the following suggestions:

1. *Surround yourself with things that stimulate your creative appetite.* In other words, books, paintings, games, collectibles, hobbies, and so on.

2. *Beyond your work, have an alternate creative pursuit.* It can be anything from sculpting, painting, writing, weaving, or designing clothes to whittling or needlepoint.

3. *Use weekends and time off to recharge your creative battery.* A simple thing like a change in pace can alter, redirect, and stimulate your creative energy. Time off is the time to experiment with new ideas and try things out at your own time and in your own way. Remember, when you're away from work, you're your own person. Take advantage of that freedom and use time wisely.

4. *No one says you shouldn't work on weekends.* If you have the urge to get something done, by all means do it. Putting in four to six hours on a weekend doesn't mean you're a workaholic.

5. *Surround yourself with people who inspire and stimulate you to think creatively.* I mean people like yourself who don't accept things at face value, who challenge ideas, and who force you to use your mind creatively. There is nothing like a hot political debate, philosophic discussion, or moral/ethical dilemma to stimulate your creative core and rouse you to action.

6. *Plan creative events.* Stay busy. No need to crawl under the

covers in your time off to hibernate. Chances are you've been sitting all week and looking for something stimulating to sink your teeth into. That's what time off is for. Now you have the opportunity to tune up your creative machinery and channel it in new directions.

7. *Use inconsequential chores as learning experiences.* A mundane chore like mowing the lawn can be a creative experience. See beyond the tedium of the chore, and look upon it as a physical and mental experience. Exercise, as you already know, is something we all need. But in the process of moving, we can also tap and explore those inner spaces in our minds that Mike Spino mentioned in his book on running, and also the experience of "aloneness" described by Dr. Freudenberger as a remedy for burn-out. In sum, commonplace chores, like mowing a lawn, painting a room, laying tile, and weeding a garden, give us the opportunity to learn more about ourselves, and to think about problems and ideas in a relaxed and nonthreatening setting.

8. *Set learning goals.* Just as you set idea goals, why not use spare time judiciously and set learning goals? That will keep you on your toes, your creative energy circulating at a steady pace. What kind of learning goals? It's up to you. If you're a history freak, it can be a scholarly learning goal, such as discovering why the Roman Empire finally collapsed, why ancient Greece was the center of a vast cultural renaissance, and so on. Or your learning goals can be of a more practical nature, such as teaching yourself to build a cabinet from scratch, learning rewiring techniques to avoid calling an electrician for small electrical problems, or learning basic tenets of landscape gardening. Setting and meeting learning goals also keeps the mind active, working, and creative.

In the final section, we'll show you how to monitor your progress.

CHAPTER 20
TRACK
YOUR
PROGRESS

What with schedules to keep, deadlines to meet, and a million and one things to do and see, we seldom stop to reflect upon it at all—to put the past, present, and future into a graspable perspective. It's easy to become overwhelmed by schedules, appointments, and commitments and to lose touch with ourselves.

An excellent way to check ourselves, to monitor and appraise our creativity, and to stimulate further creativity is to keep a journal or diary. This may seem like an incompatible chore for many because it involves pausing from time to time to review and record your thoughts. However, contrary to popular thought, it's not just scientists, writers, and lovesick schoolgirls who stand to benefit from a journal. More appropriately, it's anyone who wants to get to know himself better. There is no better way to get in touch with yourself than by recording your thoughts and observations on a regular basis. It encourages you to contemplate your creative achievements and plan still greater ones for the future.

Keeping a journal serves many purposes:

1. It permits breathing time for reflection
2. It's your personal statement. Only *you* will read and ponder the entries.
3. If used regularly and conscientiously, it will be a consoling voice when you have no one to turn to.
4. Once you get into it, you'll see that the journal is a conduit to your subconscious. Problems that plague you can be sorted out, argued over, and discussed at great length.

Let's say that you've arrived at a creative crossroads and don't know where to turn. You're confused, torn in different directions. A series of probing journal entries might help you find the answer you're looking for. Like the scientist diligently recording every step of his experiment so he can accurately assess his findings, you too can draw intelligent conclusions through the process of conscientiously monitoring yourself.

How fascinating it is to look back upon journal entries made five, ten, and fifteen years ago; what better way to profit from your mistakes and sharpen your creative faculties! The journal gives you a basis for comparison. It allows you to track your progress throughout every important step of your career, and to reflect upon your accomplishments to date.
5. Last, and most important, if used continually, it strokes, prods, and encourages creativity. Through insight, greater creative strides can be made.

How do you start? Slowly at first, until you develop a comfortable rapport and friendship with your journal. Starting can be difficult and a little awkward. Initially, you may be embarrassed by the exercise. You'll find yourself staring at blank pages, wondering how and where to begin. Follow the steps outlined below, and you'll see how easy and satisfying it can be to keep a journal.

1. *Start anywhere.* In the beginning, it's not important that you begin at a logical place. Until you're comfortable with the process of making entries, start anywhere. Soon enough, your entries

will take on a logical line of thought. Or you can create a "break the ice" format for yourself. For instance, you can begin with an overview of your work, how it went, impressions, interesting events. From there you can work toward events and insights that are of more pressing concern. Whatever warmup routine you adopt, make sure it gets your mind and emotions ready for deeper revelations and insights.

2. *Make sure a single entry is no less than a half page in length.* Anything less than that is a waste of time. Later on, when comfortable with the process, you may find that single entries run two, three, and four pages. You'll be amazed at what you can learn in the process of fleshing out a thought. Right before your eyes, an idea you've kept tucked away in the far recesses of your mind comes alive in the process of writing and thinking. Once you get into it, you'll see how exciting it can be.

3. *Get into the habit of making entries on a regular basis.* Some people make entries once a month and there are many who make entries once, twice, and several times a week. Initially, try making your journal entry every two weeks and, once comfortable with the process, try it every week.

4. *Find a comfortable time and place to devote to your journal.* Suggested times are weekends and evenings. Make sure there are no pressures or schedules to contend with. A half hour is never enough. If you're tense or nervous, it could take you a half hour just to unwind and get your thoughts in order. There is no average time for making a journal entry. It can take you fifteen minutes, and it can take you two hours. It depends on how motivated you are.

5. *Have no goals or expectations.* Approach your journal with an open mind. You're not out to prove anything, accomplish anything, or make an impression. If you must have a purpose or goal, it's simply to get insight. Through insight, important breakthroughs and discoveries can be made.

6. *Reread your journal entries regularly.* Don't make a journal entry and forget about it. Depending upon how often you make entries, get into the habit of going back and rereading entries every few months. Having studied past and present entries, you'll be equipped to forge ahead, tighten the reins, and better appraise and understand your creative core.

More personally, whenever something is troubling you, or you just want to get something off your chest, the journal is there for you. Like a loyal friend, it will never betray or reveal your private thoughts. To insure a lasting bond, all that's required is honesty.

Besides keeping a journal, it's also a good idea to stop periodically and reappraise your progress to date. The best times for reappraisal are key turning points in your life: changing jobs (or career direction), relocating, or suddenly altering your life in some way.

Just as you did a personality and skills tune-up in Part One, Chapter Six to find out if you have the social and technical skills necessary for your work, it's equally important to reevaluate those skills on a regular basis throughout your career. I suggest doing it no less than once a year, and possibly twice a year, if you feel it will help.

Start by asking yourself the following questions:

1. Am I satisfied with my work?
2. Am I realizing my goals?
3. Can any constructive changes be made? What are they?
4. Am I fully harnessing my creative energy and realizing my creative potential?

The reappraisal period can be compared to a visit to your family doctor. You'd rather put it off and deal with it another time, but your conscience and sense of responsibility tell you it's essential for your well-being. The same rationale applies to periodic reappraisals.

The idea is to remain on track, and to keep working toward your targets. Asking yourself the four questions listed above may take all of five or ten minutes, yet within that short period of time you'll appraise the progress you've made thus far.

If you're honest with yourself, you may discover you veered off course without realizing it, or made compromises you didn't intend to make. Whatever the reason, this is the time to decide on a course of action and get back on track.

If your goal is to design a pocket computer, rise through the corporate ranks, become the next Picasso, work for the best public relations firm, become a criminal attorney—this is the time to see if you're working toward those ends.

You may be delighted to discover that you've done far better than you anticipated and that this is the ideal time to do some long-range planning. How do the next ten to fifteen years look?

Finally, if you love what you're doing, and are functioning at creative capacity, you should feel pretty good about yourself. Get in touch with that feeling and enjoy it. You've accomplished something and it's worthy of celebration. You don't have to wallow in your victory, but every once in a while it's important to take pride in your work and give yourself a congratulatory pat on the back.

As we said earlier, chances are you'll never achieve perfection. But don't forget that perfection is an elusive, intangible goal. It will always be dangling in front of you, beckoning, seducing you to work just a little harder to achieve that special end.

Nevertheless, you've come a long way. Your skills are being honed, your intellectual powers are sharper, and you're learning how to wheel and deal like a pro. These are praiseworthy attributes. You've learned how to step outside yourself so you can appraise your progress to date. In essence, you've learned to be your severest critic, no easy accomplishment by any stretch of the imagination.

Maybe you've even achieved a certain amount of recognition. Fellow workers, industry leaders, family, and possibly society at large have placed your work in high esteem. Regardless of the scope of your achievements, and the number of people you reach and affect, remember that feelings of personal pride and accomplishment overshadow all else. They buoy you, propel you, and energize you to go even further. After all, how many of us *actually* realize our goals and work to full creative potential? Sadly, only a small minority. However, there is no reason why you can't be part of that select group. By now you know there is no mystery to the creative process. Don't live your life wishing you were someone else, or waiting for something to happen. You're perfect just the way you are and you have the power, energy, and creative potential to go as far as your abilities will take you. Eliminate the word *defeat* from your vocabulary. Instead, substitute *success, happiness, enrichment,* and *creative fulfillment.*

LAST WORD

A few last thoughts. At this point, I don't have to tell you what creativity can do for you. To sum up, it can change your life, make you more productive, give meaning to your life, and, finally, provide a sense of excitement and adventure that permeates everything you do. It's a word that should be part of your life. As we said in the opening chapters, it's not an exclusive word confined to certain types of work. More accurately, it is a word for everyone, and the sooner we realize this, the happier and more self-satisfied we'll be.

It doesn't matter what career path you choose. What is important is loving and being totally immersed in your work. From that, creative achievements follow.

And, no matter how involved, stimulated, or obsessed you are with achieving your goal, know when to complete a project and go on to the next. Know when you've taken an idea, project, or concept as far as it can go. No matter what you do, inevitably you reach a saturation point where you can go no further. You've reached a limit, you're at the end of the line, you've climbed the mountain and can go no further. Not an ounce of energy can be drained from your system and channeled into the project. All variables have been probed, and all approaches and arguments have been considered and explored. Like it or not, you're at the last page.

What do you do? You *stop*. For some, this is not easy. Many of us refuse to stop, and as a result we wind up beating a proverbial dead horse. Somewhere along the line we lose perspective and become obsessed with our work. No matter what we do, we're never satisfied with the results. When we can go no further, we delude ourselves into thinking there are still untapped avenues to probe. From that point on, all we're doing is repeating ourselves.

Thus, all your efforts are counterproductive. Your engine is overheating, and you're going nowhere. What was an objective exercise is now a subjective obsession. Whatever you do, learn to view your work objectively, knowing when to shut all systems and go on to the next project. At some point, pause for a few moments, reflect upon your progress, take some much deserved pride in your work, turn your desk light off, and head for the door. All the while, begin contemplating the next project.

See your work realistically. Maximize your creative potential by channeling energy in the right direction. This way your career will be punctuated by a number of brief pauses, points where goals have been reached and new ones added in their place. This way your career takes the form of a long, exciting relay race where you're hurdling one barrier after the next. Once a barrier is taken, you can look forward to charging toward the next one and chalking up another creative victory.

In conclusion, it's important that we see creativity for what it is. On an individual scale, it can transform you into a new person, give you a new sense of identity, catapult you to the very pinnacle of your career; on a larger scale it can aesthetically, intellectually, artistically, technologically, and materially enhance society. In short, it can make the world a better place in which to live. Use your creativity wisely. Use it to benefit yourself, your family, and the organization you work for, and also use it for the betterment of mankind.